Learn
LIBRARY OF CONGRESS SUBJECT ACCESS

SECOND NORTH AMERICAN EDITION

by
Jacki Ganendran
Lynn Farkas

TOTALRECALL PUBLICATIONS, INC.

TotalRecall Publications, Inc.

First published in the United States of America by Scarecrow Press, Inc. 2000
Second North American edition © DocMatrix Pty Ltd 2007

Published simultaneously by TotalRecall Publications, Inc. in the United States of America, Canada, England and other countries around the world except the Pacific Rim.

ISBN 978- 1-59095-809-4

REPRINTED UNDER SPECIAL ARRANGEMENT WITH PUBLISHER BY TOTALRECALL PUBLICATIONS, Inc.

1103 Middlecreek, Friendswood, Texas, 77546
Telephone (281) 992-3131 Fax (281) 482-5390
Email sales@totalrecallpress.com

CONTENTS

INTRODUCTION

This book covers the skills necessary for a cataloger in a library or other information agency, whether at a professional or a paraprofessional level. It is suitable for use by librarianship students in universities, and others who are studying subject cataloging by themselves, with a specific goal or as part of their continuing professional development. Since most catalogs provide some subject access, it is important for all library students and most library staff to be familiar with at least the basics. Library of Congress Subject Headings are the most widely used worldwide.

Throughout the book you will find exercises to practice and test your skills. There are answers for you to check yourself at the back of the book. You may not always agree completely with the answers given, and it is useful to check them with a teacher or experienced cataloger. Bear in mind that there is often room for more than one interpretation or emphasis, particularly in the area of subject analysis.

Library of Congress Subject Headings and their subdivisions are updated with each annual edition. This second edition reflects practices as recorded in the 28rd (2005) edition *of Library of Congress subject headings* and the online version of the *Subject cataloging manual* current in December 2006.

References have been made to the relevant section of the *Subject cataloging manual: subject headings* by way of the section numbers—e.g., H 1095 Free-Floating Subdivisions.

NOTE ON CAPITALIZATION

Titles included in the text are capitalized according to standard library cataloging practice—that is, apart from names, only the first word of the title has a capital letter. This is intended to accustom library students and staff to this style.

Chapter 1
INTRODUCTION TO SUBJECT CATALOGING

Introduction

Cataloging is the preparation of bibliographic information for catalog records.

Catalogers use a set of cataloging tools, which are the agreed international rules and standards.

Cataloging consists of

- descriptive cataloging
- subject cataloging
- classification

Subject Cataloging

Subject cataloging is the process of determining subject headings for an item. The cataloger seeks the headings that best represent the subjects of the work in words and/or phrases prescribed in an authoritative list.

Aims of Subject Cataloging

- To provide access by subject to all relevant materials
- To provide subject access to materials through all suitable principles of subject organization - i.e., matter, process, application
- To bring together all references to material on the same subject regardless of different terminology, different subject approaches, and the changing nature of the material itself
- To show affiliations among subject fields
- To provide entry at any level of analysis
- To provide entry through any vocabulary common to any considerable group of users
- To provide a formal description of the subject content of the item in the most precise terms possible, whether this be a word, phrase, class number etc
- To provide the means for the user to select from among all items in any particular category—e.g., most recent.

EXERCISE 1.1

1. What is your understanding of a

   Subject:

Subject heading:

2. Write down as many subject headings lists as you can:

Who Uses Subject Headings Lists?

- The cataloger or indexer— to allocate headings
- The searcher—to plan a search strategy—that is, to identify appropriate headings for use in searching for a particular topic. A searcher may be a library user or library staff
- The originator of the document (ideally) in order to use standard terminology.

EXERCISE 1.2

What needs do the following users have of a subject headings list?

1. Cataloger:

2. Reference advisor:

3. Library user:

4. Acquisitions officer:

5. Interlibrary loans officer:

6. Author:

Vocabulary Control

The purpose of any list of subject headings or thesaurus is to control the terms used in a catalog, bibliography or index.

Controlled Vocabulary

A controlled vocabulary uses a set of predetermined terms to represent concepts. Only one term or phrase describes each concept; alternatives such as synonyms or variant spellings are not acceptable.

A controlled vocabulary explicitly records the hierarchical and associative relations of a concept:

e.g., Allergy
Narrower term: Hay fever

It establishes the size or scope of each topic:

e.g., Baseball
includes the concept softball

It identifies synonymous terms and selects one preferred term:

e.g., Capsicum
Use: Peppers

For homonyms, it explicitly identifies the multiple concepts expressed by that word or phrase:

e.g., Springs (mechanical devices)
vs
Springs (water sources)

Library of Congress Subject Headings (LCSH) is one example of a controlled list.

Thesaurus

A subject list that includes hierarchical relationships between headings is also called a thesaurus.

Uncontrolled Vocabulary

An uncontrolled vocabulary uses the actual words in a document as an access point. It is also referred to as natural language, or free text vocabulary.

Terms may be selected from the text or the title.

EXERCISE 1.3

1. List examples of systems that use

   Controlled vocabulary:

   Uncontrolled vocabulary:

2. What are the advantages and disadvantages of controlled and uncontrolled vocabulary?

   Controlled vocabulary
   Advantages:

   Disadvantages:

   Uncontrolled vocabulary
   Advantages:

   Disadvantages:

Pre-coordinate and Post-coordinate Indexing

Pre-coordination

In a pre-coordinate system, the parts of a heading are put together (pre-coordinated) by the cataloger or indexer to create a specific subject heading. Terms are put together in a specific pre-determined order.

To retrieve documents from the system, the searcher must use the same terms in the search strategy. This requires the searcher to put together the heading in the same form as constructed by the cataloger. There is no opportunity for the searcher to combine concepts in a search at the retrieval stage. (In some systems, search capabilities allowing each part of the subject heading to be accessed, act in a "post-coordinate" way).

In LCSH, for example,

Title	Laws concerning the transporting of coal in Australia
Heading	Coal—Transportation—Law and legislation—Australia

At the very least, the searcher needs to know what the subject heading begins with.

Post-coordination

In a post-coordinate system, the cataloger may use several terms to cover all subjects.
The searcher can then search using Boolean operators (and, not, or) to construct the search.
The searcher need not be aware of all the terms used and there is no order of terms involved.

e.g.,	Title	Laws concerning the transporting of coal in Australia
	Headings	Coal
		Laws or Legislation
		Transport or Transporting or Transportation
		Australia

The searcher will find this item by using any (or any combination) of the subject terms.

EXERCISE 1.4 - SYNONYMS

1. What is a synonym?

2. What tools could you use to identify synonyms?

3. Provide synonyms for the following words or phrases:

	Term	Synonym(s)
1.	author	______________
2.	stamp collecting	______________
3.	car	______________
4.	monograph	______________
5.	trailer	______________
6.	serial	______________
7.	hiking	______________
8.	saturated	______________
9.	slack	______________
10.	corpulence	______________
11.	elevators	______________
12.	hirsute	______________
13.	shore	______________
14.	rage	______________
15.	hemp	______________

EXERCISE 1.5 - HOMONYMS

1. What is a homonym?

2. What tools could you use to identify homonyms?

3. Provide two possible meanings for each of the following terms:

	Term	Meanings
1.	slack	1. ______
		2. ______
2.	slam	1. ______
		2. ______
3.	toast	1. ______
		2. ______
4.	lag	1. ______
		2. ______
5.	cuff	1. ______
		2. ______

Subject Analysis

Subject analysis involves several steps:

1. First, examine the work in hand.
2. Then decide on several keywords that could represent the subject.
3. Using the keywords as a starting point, go to each term in the list to identify appropriate headings.

EXERCISE 1.6

Comprehension and Summarizing

Choose the statement that best expresses the main idea of the following paragraphs. More than one answer in each group may be correct. You are trying to find the best answer.

1. The writing of political comments on walls seems to me to be justified, then, as long as they contain messages that would not otherwise reach the people, and as long as the writers of these comments have no regular access to other media, such as newspapers or television. I only wish, though, that they would confine their aerosol activities to walls, and stop defacing public monuments and statues.

   The writer approves of political graffiti only if they
   a. attack the government
   b. are written so that everyone can understand them
   c. do not compete with the media (e.g., the press and television)
   d. contain useful or important information.

2. Most of us lead unhealthy lives : we spend far too much time sitting down. If, in addition, we are careless about our diets, our bodies soon become flabby and our systems sluggish. Then the guilt feelings start: "I must go on a diet", "I must try to lose weight", "I must get more fresh air and exercise", "I must stop smoking", "I must try to keep fit". There are some aspects of our unhealthy lives that we cannot avoid. I am thinking of such features of modern urban life as pollution, noise, rushed meals and stress. But keeping fit is a way to minimise the effects of these evils.

   Yoga, as practised in the West, is the most widely known and popular of the systems for achieving the necessary state of relaxation. Contrary to popular belief, you do not have to learn a lot of strange words or become a Buddhist in order to benefit from Yoga. It seems ironical, though, that as our lives have improved in a material sense, we have found it increasingly necessary to go back to forms of activity—physical effort on the one hand, and relaxation on the other—which were the natural way of our forefathers.

   Unfitness is the result of
   a. lack of fresh air and exercise
   b. overeating, smoking and living in towns
   c. not eating properly and not getting enough exercise
   d. not taking part in sports.

   Pollution, noise and stress are examples of
   a. causes of unfitness
   b. bad features of living in towns
   c. the things we must avoid if we are to stay healthy
   d. industrial life and work.

   Our reaction to being out of condition is to
   a. give up smoking and go on a diet
   b. start a programme of keep-fit exercises
   c. make resolutions to lead a healthier life
   d. take up a sport.

   Many people believe that in order to practise yoga
   a. you must learn a special vocabulary
   b. it is better to become a Buddhist
   c. you must learn to relax completely
   d. you must wear special clothing.

   Our forefathers were healthy because
   a. their way of life involved both exercise and relaxation
   b. they were careful to get plenty of fresh air and keep fit
   c. they lived in the country and spent time out of doors
   d. they had simple work to do and very little to worry about.

   List 4-5 keywords that describe important concepts/ideas/points contained in the passage.

   Summarize the passage in one sentence.

Determining the Subject

First, examine the item to decide on topics. You should make this decision based on the evidence in the book in hand, not on what you know or think about the topic.

Then, find correct headings to describe the topics. To decide on topics, examine:

• title	may or may not be helpful
• subtitle	is often more useful
• author	may provide an indication of the broad topic if the author has published in the area
• foreword, preface, introduction	usually state the author's intention
• publisher	may give an indication if the publisher specialises in a particular subject area
• series	may be useful
• table of contents,index and list of illustrations	are usually good indicators of the main topics
• text	can be used to confirm your ideas about the subject, skim text and read a sample
• cataloging-in-publication	useful but use with care, as CIPs are prepared prior to publication, often without the work in hand

Example

When
Your Partner
Dies

Mary Mortimer

Hale & Iremonger

(title page)

Contents

Preface

I have written this book in an attempt to make sense of the two major tragedies in my life - the deaths of two partners, each of whom I loved deeply. These deaths, and that of a dear friend, are my main personal experiences of bereavement. I have therefore focused on the death of a partner, although I am strongly aware of the devastation which can result from the death of a parent or a child.

When we lose a parent, and especially both parents, we lose the generation 'above' us, the source of our life, our early knowledge of the world, so many of our characteristics and attitudes.

When our child dies, at whatever age, we are stunned by the unnatural order of events. We do not expect to survive our children: our hopes are for their future, even more than our own.

With the death of a partner, on the other hand, we lose the person who shares our everyday life, who is there for breakfast and dinner, with whom we share a home, a bed, many of our hopes and fears, memories and future plans. So the loss affects every aspect of our lives, and requires the most pervasive practical and emotional adjustments.

There are other books which present a more academic or professional approach to bereavement. I have written from my own experience - and that of close friends whose grief I have shared. I have been able to draw conclusions about the common aspects of grieving, and the different effects of sudden and of expected death. I try to offer practical suggestions for dealing with situations you may not yet have encountered.

Since I am a very practical person, and control over my life is of great importance to me, I emphasise what can be done in coping with the loss of a partner and its aftermath. You may find it easier than I did to let things happen, to accept this massive disruption to your physical and emotional life. I hope, however, that you will find my descriptions of events and feelings reassuring and helpful. One of our most valuable sources of support in times of crisis is the knowledge that our experience is not unique, and that others have felt or behaved in a similar way.

For most couples who are still together, one will have to live through and beyond the death of the other. Yet death is perhaps the last remaining taboo. Not only do we not talk about it, we don't even call it by name. We prefer to say that 'the deceased' or the 'dearly departed' or the 'loved one' has 'passed away', 'gone', 'left us', 'gone to Heaven', is 'at rest' or 'at peace'; we talk around the event without using the words. By not naming death and dying, we deny the reality and make it more difficult for those who are close to it to share and express their sadness, their anxiety and their anger.

Many people who have no personal experience of death and loss, feel inadequate when a friend is bereaved. In their embarrassment they try to ignore this momentous event, and in so doing they add to their friend's feelings of hurt and isolation.

If you believe in a God or gods, and a life after death, I am sure it can be a great source of comfort and strength. I hope you do not turn away from your belief in your anger and feeling of betrayal. 'Why me?" is a very common reaction to tragedy. Though I do not believe in God or Heaven, I do have great faith in humankind: in our capacity to love and help each other, to share and give meaning to our joys and our sorrows. When I have felt most desolate, I have often asked 'Why me?" Perhaps part of the answer lies in this book.

National Library of Australia Cataloging-in-publication entry

Mortimer, Mary, 1944-

When your partner dies.

Bibliography.
ISBN 0 86806 417 3.
ISBN 0 86806 418 1 (pbk.)

1. Widowhood. 2. Bereavement. 3. Widows—Life skill guides.
4. Widowers—Life skill guides. I. Title

155.937 086 54

For *When your partner dies*, the technical examination provides this overview:

• title	Provides a lot of information. This book is clearly about what happens when a partner dies
• subtitle	Not applicable
• author	Not helpful

• foreword, preface, introduction	Preface explains content and author's intention
• publisher	Not helpful
• series	Not applicable
• contents and index	Contents confirm the subject of work, including practical nature
• text	Also confirms the subject
• cataloging-in-publication	Useful, though some headings are not in common use

Principles of Subject Cataloging

User

The subject cataloger should always consider users and their needs. The heading, in wording and structure, should be one that the user would be most likely to look for.

Uniform Headings

Try to ensure uniform headings. All items dealing with one subject should be placed under one heading.

Terminology

The aim is always to match the user's term with the heading in the catalog. Several problems arise, since you must choose among:

- synonyms
- variant spellings
- English vs other languages
- technical vs popular terms
- obsolete vs current terms
- homonyms.

Direct Entry

Ideally, identify a heading that directly describes the subject:

e.g., Cats
not
Mammals—Domestic animals—Cats

EXERCISE 1.7

Investigate the subject headings you would need to use to find information on the following topics. Use two different types of libraries. Try to select two libraries that serve different clientele. Make a note if you are unable to find any material on a topic in your library of choice. Why might this be?

Topic	Library 1	Library 2
1. National parks in Canada		
2. Building in tropical conditions		
3. Smoking and health		
4. Library classification schemes		
5. Fitting a jacket		
6. Women in business		
7. Desktop publishing		
8. Marketing your services		
9 The Second World War		
10. Cataloging nonbook materials		
11. Presentation skills for new teachers		
12. Australian photographers		

Chapter 2
INTRODUCTION TO LIBRARY OF CONGRESS SUBJECT HEADINGS (LCSH)

LCSH is an accumulation of subject headings established by the Library of Congress since 1898. The *List of subject headings for use in dictionary catalogs*, prepared by a committee of the American Library Association and published in 1895, was used as the basis for the Library's own list of subject headings.

The first edition of the Library of Congress list was printed in parts between 1909 and 1914. The title changed to *Library of Congress subject headings* with the eighth edition in 1975.

Headings are created as needed when works are cataloged for the collections of the Library of Congress. Headings are also retained in new editions of the list regardless of the recency or frequency of the list.

Inconsistencies in the formulation of headings can often be explained by the policies in force at the varying dates of their creation. LCSH is also an extremely large list, to which many catalogers and groups of catalogers contribute.

Versions

Library of Congress subject headings are available in the following formats:

- *Library of Congress subject headings*—the printed version
- *Classification Web*—Web access to LC Classification and LC Subject Headings
- *Library of Congress authorities*—online at authorities.loc.gov (This version does not include headings combined with free-floating subdivisions, or instructions for use of geographic subdivisions.)

Additional Publications

LCSH contains main headings, some subdivisions and references. Library of Congress policies and instructions on using LCSH are found in the *Subject cataloging manual: subject headings.* It is essential to use the manual to ensure correct usage and to have access to additional subdivisions.

The following are also published by the Library of Congress, and contain information about changes:

- *Cataloging service bulletin*—a quarterly update of policy, headings and subdivisions
- *Free-floating subdivisions: an alphabetical index*—an annual index of all free-floating subdivisions
- *LC period subdivisions under names of places*
- *LC subject headings weekly lists*—new and revised headings, available online at www.loc.gov/aba/cataloging/subject/weeklylists/
- *Library of Congress subject headings: principles of structure and policies for application*—a concise overview/introduction to the principles used to establish and apply LC subject headings.

Types of Headings Found in LCSH

Topical headings and subdivisions including types of objects and concepts
- disciplines
- methods and procedures
- activities
- industries
- classes of people

Jurisdictional geographic names

Non-jurisdictional geographic names including geographic features
- areas and regions
- trails, parks and reserves
- city sections
- early cities, empires, kingdoms

Names of persons incapable of authorship and families including
- legendary, mythological and fictitious characters
- gods
- dynasties
- royal houses

Names of **art works**

Names of **chemicals, drugs and minerals; biological names**

Other proper names including
- languages
- computer languages and systems
- ethnic groups
- roads
- structures and buildings
- events
- trade names
- games.

Structure of Subject Headings (H 180)

Subject headings may take several forms:
- Single word—e.g., Dams
- Multiple words, direct heading—e.g., Data transmission systems
- Inverted heading—e.g., Art, Medieval
- Phrase heading—e.g., Photography of birds
- Complex phrases—e.g., Infants switched at birth
- Subdivided heading—e.g., Libraries–Security measures
- Qualified terms—e.g., Seals (Animals)

Arrangement of LCSH

LCSH headings authorized for use as subject entries are printed in bold type in the printed version of LCSH. Authorized subdivisions are also printed in bold type. Subdivisions appear under the LCSH heading following a long dash, without repeating the heading. If two or more subdivisions are used, the main heading and the preceding subdivisions are replaced by additional long dashes:

e.g., **Libraries**
— Public relations *(May Subd Geog)*
UF Public relations – Libraries *[Former heading]*
— — Awards *(May Subd Geog)*
— — — United States
NT John Cotton Dana Library Public Relations Award

This heading would appear in a library catalog as:
Libraries—Public relations—Awards—United States

The following symbols are used to codify the relationship between headings:

UF Used For
BT Broader Topic
RT Related Topic
SA See Also
NT Narrower Topic
USE Use

(May Subd Geog) Place names may follow the heading or subdivision.
(Not Subd Geog) The Library of Congress has decided not to subdivide by place.

Headings without either designation have not yet been considered for geographic subdivision. They may not currently be subdivided by place. As headings are constantly being reviewed, their status may change.

If the notation *(May Subd Geog)* appears a number of times in a subject heading sequence, insert the place name after the last subdivision containing the notation. (See **Geographic Subdivisions** in Chapter 4 for more details of the use of this notation.)

Scope notes are provided to ensure consistency of usage. A scope note:

- specifies the range of subject matter to which a heading should be applied
- draws necessary distinctions between related headings
- states which of several meanings is the one to use.

EXERCISE 2.1

Study the following extract from LCSH, and answer the questions below:

Beverage industry *(May Subd Geog)*
UF Drink industry
BT Food industry and trade
RT Bottling
NT Alcoholic beverage industry
Bottled water industry
Brewing industry
Carbonated beverage industry
Chicory beverage industry
Cider industry
Coffee industry
Distilling industries
Fruit drink industry
Fruit juice industry
Mineral water industry
Non-alcoholic beverage industry
Rooibos tea industry
Soft drink industry
Tea trade
— Employees
— — Labor unions *(May Subd Geog)*
— Equipment and supplies
NT Beverage processing machinery
Beverage managers, Hotel
USE Hotel beverage managers
Beverage processing plants
(May Subd Geog)
BT Food processing plants
NT Breweries
Distilleries
Milk plants
Wineries
— Equipment and supplies
NT Beverage processing machinery

1. Write down all authorized headings, ignoring the subdivisions. Do not include broader and narrower terms.

2. Write down all possible headings with subdivisions. Ignore geographic subdivisions.

3. Using **United States** as the place name, write down all possible headings with geographic subdivisions.

References (H 373)

LCSH contains cross-references that represent a mix of philosophies prevalent at different times in the history of the list. (This explains why cross-referencing practices are not consistent within the list.)

USE (or SEE) References

USE references are made from **unauthorized** or **non-preferred** terms to an **authorized** or **preferred** heading. Under the preferred heading, there is a code UF that precedes the headings not used. For example,

Cars (Automobiles)
USE Automobiles

Automobiles
UF Cars (Automobiles)

That is, **Automobiles** is the preferred term, and **Cars (Automobiles)** is the non-preferred term.

USE references are made from synonyms, variant spellings, variant forms of expression, alternate constructions of headings and older forms of headings. USE references may be used even when the heading and unused words are not synonymous.

Older catalogs may use the word SEE instead of USE.

References Indicating Hierarchical Relationships (H 370)

LCSH links subject headings in order to show the relationship between **broader** (**BT**) and **narrower** (**NT**) headings. This allows a user to make a search more general or more specific.
The relationship is always reciprocal, e.g.,

Exterior lighting
BT Lighting

Lighting
NT Exterior lighting

A heading is normally linked to the one immediately next to it in the subject heading hierarchy (either immediately upwards/broader or immediately lower/narrower).

The following relationships are considered hierarchical:

Genus/species
Apes
BT Primates

Whole/part
Toes
BT Foot

Instance (or generic topic/proper-named example)
Whitewater Lake (Wis.)
BT Lakes—Wisconsin
[Whitewater Lake is an instance of a lake in Wisconsin]

References Indicating Associated Relationships

LCSH also indicates relationships that are not broader or narrower but which are related. For example,

Ornithology
RT Birds

Birds
RT Ornithology

While there is no hierarchical relationship, terms are mentally associated to such an extent that the link reveals alternative headings that might be of interest.

General References (H 371)

A general reference is made not to a specific heading but to an entire group of headings, frequently listing one or more headings as an example. This occurs because it is impractical to list all possible headings. For example,

Ethnic groups
SA *individual ethnic groups,* e.g., Hopi Indians

They can be made from a generic heading to a group of headings beginning with the same word, e.g.,

Chemistry
SA *headings beginning with the word* Chemical

Sometimes they lead to subdivisions, e.g.,

Economic history
SA *subdivision* Economic conditions *under names of countries, cities,* etc.

Sometimes general USE references can be made, e.g.,

Access control
USE *subdivision* Access control *under types of archives, records, computers, computer networks, and statistical and data-gathering services, e.g.*
Computers—Access control; Psychiatric records—Access control

EXERCISE 2.2

Use this extract from LCSH to answer the questions below:

Artisans *(May Subd Geog)*
UF Artizans
Craftsmen
BT Skilled labor
RT Cottage industries
NT Apprentices
Basket makers
Diamond cutters

What is the relationship between

1. **Artisans** and **Craftsmen**

2. **Artisans** and **Apprentices**

3. **Artisans** and **Skilled labor**

4. **Artisans** and **Cottage industries**

5. Is **Craftsmen** an authorized / permitted term?

EXERCISE 2.3

Use LCSH to determine if these are acceptable headings. If not, write down the correct term.

	Subject heading	Correct heading
1.	Felix the Cat	______________
2.	Guitar—Construction	______________
3.	Fusion reactors—Fuels	______________
4.	Fusion reactors—Germany	______________
5.	Semi-conductors	______________
6.	Guitar and harp music	______________
7.	Heliophobus plants	______________
8.	Seychelles—Coup d'etat, 1977	______________
9.	Coups d'etat—Seychelles	______________
10.	Tempo	______________

Chapter 3
ASSIGNING SUBJECT HEADINGS (H 180)

General Guidelines

General Rule

Assign one or more subject headings that best summarize the overall contents of the work. The aim is to provide access to the most important topics.

Number of Headings

This will vary with the work being cataloged. Generally, a maximum of 6 headings is appropriate. If more than one heading is used, arrange the headings in order of their predominance in the work.

Order of Headings

- Assign the heading that represents the predominant topic of the work as the first subject heading.
- If a work has two equally important major topics, assign them one after the other, before any headings for secondary topics.
- Assign headings for secondary topics in any order following the headings for the major topics.

Specificity

Assign the most specific heading that represents exactly the contents of the work.

e.g., **Mathematics** and **Trigonometry** are not normally assigned to the same work.

Where a specific heading is not possible, assign a heading that is broader or more general than the topic.

Works On a Single Topic

Assign the one heading that represents exactly the contents of the work.

e.g.,	Title	The world within the tide pool
	Subject heading	**Tide pool ecology**

Subtopic Not Normally Subsumed Under a Heading

Normally a work on a single topic can be expected to cover a range of subtopics. If, within such a work, there is a subtopic that falls outside the scope of the expected range, allocate headings for the main topic plus an additional heading for the subtopic. The subtopic should cover at least 20% of the work to warrant a separate heading.

e.g.,	Title	Notes on planning and managing agricultural operations in Godavari
	Subject headings	1. **Agriculture—India—Godavari—Statistics** 2. **Rice—India—Godavari**

Multi-Topic Works

For works on more than one topic treated separately, assign headings to bring out each concept individually

e.g., Title Bibliography on snow, ice and frozen ground
Subject headings **1. Snow—Bibliography**
2. Ice—Bibliography
3. Frozen ground—Bibliography

Hierarchical Considerations

Special guidelines apply for related topics that fit under a common theme within a work.

Two or three related topics in a work

If a heading exists that represents precisely the two or three topics, assign it and not the two or three headings.

e.g., Title The distinctive excellences of Greek and Latin
Subject heading **1. Classical literature**
(Separate headings are not used because Classical literature includes both Greek and Latin and nothing else)

Rule of three

If a broad heading exists, but includes more than the two or three topics in question, assign the two or three headings, not the broader heading.

e.g., Title Travels in Brazil, Ecuador and Peru
Subject headings **1. Brazil—Description and travel**
2. Ecuador—Description and travel
3. Peru—Description and travel
(not the more inclusive South America)

Rule of four (four or more related topics in a work)

Do not assign a separate heading for each topic where a single heading that covers all topics can be used.

If no such heading exists, assign separate headings to four, or, if more than four, assign several very comprehensive headings or a single form heading. For example, a work on hot rods, go-karts, dragsters, sprint cars and Formula One cars should be assigned the heading

Automobiles, Racing

Multi-Element Works

If a work treats a single subject from different aspects or contains various elements of one topic, use one pre-coordinated heading, if there is one available.

e.g., Title Chemical plant management in the U.S.
Subject heading **1. Chemical plants—United States—Management**

However there are many subjects that are much more complex with no pre-coordinated heading available for use. In this case bring out each concept individually.

e.g., Title — A method of setting up the eigenvalue problem for the linear, shallow-water wave equation for irregular bodies of water with variable water depth and application to bays and harbors in Hawai'i.

Subject headings
1. **Ocean waves**
2. **Eigenvalues**
3. **Oceanography—Data processing**
4. **Bays—Hawaii**
5. **Harbors—Hawaii**

Principle Versus a Specific Case

If a work discusses a principle and illustrates the principle by referring to a specific case, assign a heading for the principle and also a heading for the specific case, if appropriate. For example, a work on the anatomy of vertebrates that illustrates this by reference to cats would get two subject headings, one for the main topic and one for the example.

Title — The anatomy of vertebrates

Subject headings
1. **Vertebrates—Anatomy**
2. **Cats—Anatomy**

Viewpoint of Author or Publisher

Always consider this and assign a heading if useful.

e.g., If the work is written primarily for a juvenile audience use the subdivision **—Juvenile literature**

If a general textbook is intended for specific persons, allocate a heading for the topic and one for the special interest or application.

e.g., Title — Psychology for nurses

Subject headings
1. **Psychology**
2. **Nursing—Psychological aspects**

Concepts in Titles

Titles and subtitles are important because they sometimes state in the words of the author or publisher the subject matter of the work. Bring out each topic so identified if it is discussed in the work.

Title — Easy-to-make wooden candlesticks, chandeliers and lamps

Subject headings
1. **Woodwork**
2. **Candlesticks**
3. **Chandeliers**
4. **Lamps**

Additional Aspects

Place

If a work involves a specific geographic area, bring out the area by a subject heading or a subdivision.

Time

Express the chronological aspects significant to the contents of the work in situations where the Library of Congress subject heading system allows it.

Named entities

Assign headings from the name authority file or subject authority file for individual persons, families, corporate bodies, projects etc. that are significant to the content of the work.

Form

Assign form headings and subdivisions to represent what the item itself is—that is, its format or the particular type or arrangement of data that it contains—in situations where headings or subdivisions for these types of materials exist.

Form Subject Headings

Form refers to the manner or style in which material is presented, the particular character or method of presentation of information (e.g., Aerial photographs, Biography, Catalogs and collections, Dictionaries, Encyclopedias, Musical settings, Programmed instruction).

Form can be designated by

- a topical subject heading with form subdivision

or

- a form subject heading.

Assign form subject headings to

- works produced in a particular format for users with disabilities
  e.g., **Large type books** (often used for fiction in large print)
  Talking books (works reproduced on tape, disc or record for the visually impaired)

- rare books. If a work is held for its quality, uniqueness, or particular characteristics as a physical entity, a form subject to highlight this can be used.
  e.g., **Book ornamentation**
  Bookbinding
  Chapbooks
  Early printed books
  Fine books
  Small press books

If a Subject Heading is the Same as Another Access Point

Subject headings fulfil a different role from other access points—author, title, corporate body and so on. Therefore, name subject headings should always be assigned to reflect the subject being discussed, even if the name is also used as a title or author access point.

e.g.,

Title	The operation of the American Red Cross: an official viewpoint
Author entry	**I. American Red Cross**
Subj heading	**1. American Red Cross**

EXERCISE 3.1

Using LCSH, provide a subject heading that best represents the following topics:

Topic	Subject heading
1. The sea	__________
2. Adoption services	__________
3. Adriatic Islands	__________
4. Children as actors	__________
5. Ways of monitoring fetal heart rate	__________
6. The impact of highway traffic sounds	__________
7. Oceanic drilling ships in the Atlantic	__________
8. Catalan political satire	__________
9. An introduction to prehistoric agriculture	__________
10. The wonders of horseradish	__________

EXERCISE 3.2

Using LCSH, provide a subject heading that best represents the following topics. In some instances, the answer may require more than on heading:

Topic	Subject heading
1. Morris West's slide collections	__________
2. Water conservation and irrigation efficiency	__________
3. Cartoon-makers	__________
4. Electric condensers	__________
5. Music for organ and flute	__________
6. Sulky racing	__________
7. Harmony on the keyboard	__________
8. Prehistoric cartography	__________
9. The benefits of asparaginic acid	__________
10. Bakery products	__________

Chapter 4
MARC

Coding Subject Headings

In MARC 21, fields 600-662 (with the exception of field 653) contain subject headings or access terms that provide subject access to a bibliographic record. The following fields are of particular interest to us when MARC coding Library of Congress Subject Headings.

Note: all fields are repeatable.

600	Personal Name	This field is used for materials where a person is the subject, such as a biography. The author of a work will go into a 100 or 700 field
610	Corporate Name	This field is used for materials where an organization is the subject of the item. Corporate bodies that are authors of a work would go into 110 or 710
611	Meeting Name	This field is used for works about a conference or meeting, not for the conference proceedings. For conference proceedings, the conference name would go into 111 or 711
630	Uniform Title	This field is used for the titles of the work that is discussed in the item
648	Chronological Term	This field is used for a chronological term—e.g., a date
650	Topical Term	This field is for the topic of the work. Use the authorized form of the subject
651	Geographic Name	This field is used when a work is about a place

The second indicator specifies the source of the subject heading. For Library of Congress Subject Headings, these are identified by "0" as the second indicator.

Subfield codes for the relevant subdivisions are:

- $v Form subdivision
- $x General subdivision
- $y Chronological subdivision
- $z Geographic subdivision

The dash (--) that precedes a general subdivision is not carried in the MARC record. It may be generated based on the presence of subfields $v, $x, $y, $z.

Note on usage, from *Subject cataloguing manual: subject headings*, H1075, 1d: "Code a form subdivision as an $x subfield when it represents a form that the item is about. This often occurs when a subdivision that is normally a form subdivision is followed by another form subdivision."

For example,
Canada$vMaps (for actual maps of Canada)
But
Canada$xMaps$vBibliography (for a bibliography of maps of Canada)

Examples

Name subject headings 600, 610, 611

Model 600_0 $aPersonal name$xsubject subdivision
610_0 $aCorporate name$xsubject subdivision
611_0 $aConference name$xsubject subdivision

600 10 $aDepardieu, Gerard,$d1948-

600 10 $aChristie, Agatha,$d1890-1976$vHandbooks, manuals, etc.

610 20 $aRutgers University$xHistory

610 20 $aNASA Advisory Council.$bSolar System Exploration Committee

611 10 $aSymposium on Carcinogenesis, Mechanisms of Action,$cLondon,$d1959

611 20 $aCongress$d(1814-1815 :$cVienna).

Uniform title subject heading 630

Model 630_0 $aUniform title$xsubject subdivision

630 00 $aMicrosoft Excel (Computer file)

630 00 $aLinux$vPeriodicals

630 00 $aBible$xInfluence$xSlavic civilization.

630 00 $aLos Angeles times$vIndexes$vPeriodicals

Topical subject heading 650

Model 650_0 $aTopical subject$xsubject subdivision$zgeographic subdivision $ychronological subdivision$vform subdivision

The order of elements in topical subject headings usually follows the order shown above. It will sometimes vary depending on how the subjects are authorized to be subdivided. This is particularly so for geographic subdivisions which follow the last subject heading or subdivision that can be subdivided geographically.

Note that subjects can have geographic subdivisions in 650 subfield $z if there is a place aspect to a topic.

650 _0 $aReal estate business$xTechnological innovations$zUnited States.

650 _0 $aInternet marketing$zUnited States.

650 _0 $aMacadamia nut industry$zHawaii$xHistory

650 _0 $aAuthors, American$y20th century$vBiography

650 _0 $aDetective and mystery stories, English$xStories, plots, etc.$vHandbooks, manuals, etc.

650 _0 $aTechnology$xSocial aspects$vCongresses.

650 _0 $aSpace vehicles$xAuxiliary power supply$xCongresses

650 _0 $aArchives$zUnited States$xDirectories

650 _0 $aJapanese Americans$zCalifornia$vNewspapers

Geographic subject heading 651

Model 651 _0 $aGeographic subject heading$xsubject subdivision$ychronological subdivision$vform subdivision

651 _0 $aDenver (Colo.)$vNewspapers)

651 _0 $aLos Angeles (Calif.)

651 _0 $aColorado$xDescription and travel

651 _0 $aRocky Mountains

651 _0 $aNile River

651 _0 $aAlaska$xBoundaries$zCanada

651 _0 $aSpeedway (Ind.)$xMaps

651 _0 $aUnited States$xPolitics and government$y1853-1857

EXERCISES

Answers to many of the exercises in the following chapters are given in MARC format. You are encouraged to practice coding up as many of these as you can.

Relevant MARC codes are provided at the back of this book.

Chapter 5
SUBDIVISIONS

Introduction

Subdivisions are used extensively in LCSH. They allow a number of different concepts to be combined in a single subject heading. Subdivisions serve two functions in LCSH:

- They make a subject more specific
- They may be used to sub-arrange a large number of items under one heading in a catalog.

Some subdivisions are printed in the list but these represent only a small fraction of possible combinations of headings and subdivisions. Others may be applied as instructed in the *Library of Congress subject cataloging manual.*

Authority to use subdivisions under a particular heading can be found in four places:

1. under the subject heading in its alphabetical place in the list
2. under the general subject heading that represents the subdivision you want
3. under the list of Free-Floating Subdivisions (this does not imply uncontrolled use)
4. under a Pattern Heading.

Types of Subdivisions

There are four types of subdivisions, **topical, form, chronological** and **geographic**. Detailed instructions for assigning them appear in various sections of the *Manual.*

Topical Subdivisions

These are used to limit the concept expressed by the heading to a special subtopic.

e.g., **Corn—Harvesting**
Automobiles—Motors—Carburetors

Form Subdivisions

These indicate the form in which the material on a subject is organized and presented. They are added as the last element in the string of terms. Form subdivisions can generally be used under any topic and are not usually listed. Most form subdivisions are indicated by a general *see also* reference under the heading representing the form as a whole.

e.g., **Periodicals**
SA *subdivision* Periodicals *under specific subjects* e.g., Engineering—Periodicals.

Detailed guidance on the use of form subdivisions is given in the *Manual* (H 1075).

Chronological or Period Subdivisions

These are used to limit a heading to a particular time period. These subdivisions may:

- denote chronological sequences under countries
  e.g., **Great Britain—History—George VI, 1936-1952**

- mark significant dates in the evolution of a subject
  e.g., **Philosophy, French—18th century**

- divide arbitrarily a large file by date of publication
  e.g., **Mathematics—1961-**
  Aeronautics—Early works to 1900

EXERCISE 5.1

Using LCSH, allocate suitable subject headings to the following. Include one or more subdivisions to make your heading more specific.

Topic	Subject heading
1. The cost of constructing railroads	______________________
2. Extensions to buildings	______________________
3. Synthesis in organic chemistry	______________________
4. Data processing in credit bureaus	______________________
5. The rights and wages of employees in credit unions	______________________
6. John Brown's raid on Harpers Ferry	______________________
7. The 1929 depression in Chicago	______________________
8. The diagnosis of unipolar depression	______________________
9. Renaissance engraving	______________________
10. Hunting with bows and arrows	______________________

Multiple Subdivisions

A multiple subdivision is a subdivision in LCSH that is used to suggest the creation of similar subdivisions under the heading. It is indicated by terms in square brackets generally followed by the word "etc."

The presence of a multiple subdivision under a heading automatically gives free-floating status to similar subdivisions under the same heading, and, if the heading is a pattern heading, under those headings that it controls, e.g.,

World War, 1939-1945—Personal narratives, American, [French, German, etc.]

Possible headings are

World War, 1939-1945—Personal narratives, American
World War, 1939-1945—Personal narratives, French
World War, 1939-1945—Personal narratives, German
World War, 1939-1945—Personal narratives, Australian

The functional equivalent of a multiple subdivision may be presented in the form of a scope note, e.g.,

Solar eclipses
Subdivided by date, e.g., Solar eclipses—1854

EXERCISE 5.2

Using LCSH, provide a subject heading for each of the following:

Topic	Subject heading
1. Religious aspects of animal experiments from the Islamic viewpoint	________________
2. Subject headings for astronomy	________________
3. Christian beliefs about salt	________________
4. German words and phrases in the English Language	________________
5. Buddhist aspects of codependency	________________

Geographic Subdivisions (H 830)

These may be added when the designation *(May Subd Geog)* appears after a heading or subdivision. The designation *(Not Subd Geog)* after a heading or subdivision indicates that the Library of Congress has made a decision not to subdivide by place. Headings without either designation may currently not be subdivided by place because they have yet to be reviewed to determine whether a geographic subdivision is possible or desirable.

Below is an LC subject heading and some of its subdivisions as set out in LCSH 28th edition. If a heading contains both a geographic subdivision and a topical or form subdivision, the location of the geographic subdivision depends on which elements can be divided by place.

Remember, if a geographic subdivision is allowable in two or more places in the sequence, choose the last.

LCSH Entry

Architecture, Domestic *(May Subd Geog)*
  UF Domestic architecture
  BT Architecture
  NT A-frame houses
    Courtyard houses
    and so on . . .
  – **African influences**
  – **Conservation and restoration** *(May Subd Geog)*
  – **Mission style**
  – **Shingle style** *(May Subd Geog)*

Please note that this entry is not complete! See LCSH for the full list of headings.

Subject Headings Generated

Architecture, Domestic
Architecture, Domestic – United States
Architecture, Domestic – African influences
Architecture, Domestic – Conservation and restoration
Architecture, Domestic – Conservation and restoration – United States
Architecture, Domestic – Mission style
Architecture, Domestic – United States – Mission style
Architecture, Domestic – Shingle style
Architecture, Domestic – Shingle style – United States

EXERCISE 5.3

Here is an LCSH entry:

Banks and banking *(May Subd Geog)*
...
—**Automation**
——**Equipment and supplies**
—**Data processing**
——**Contracting out** *(May Subd Geog)*
...
—**Government ownership** *(May Subd Geog)*
——**Law and legislation** *(May Subd Geog)*

Write out all possible subdivisions, using **Canada** as a geographic subdivision.

e.g., Banks and banking—Canada

EXERCISE 5.4

Are these headings correct? If not, indicate a possible correct heading.

Topic	Subject heading
1. Parachutes—Testing—Equipment—Certification—United States	______
2. Scientific apparatus and instruments—Conservation and restoration	______
3. United States—Climate—Measurement	______
4. Birthparents—Identification—Case studies	______
5. Chamber music—Early works to 1800—England	______
6. Murderers—Civil rights—Boston (Mass.)	______
7. Trade-unions—Accounting—Law and Legislation—Michigan	______
8. Tuberculosis vaccines—Maine--Bangor	______
9. Tuberculosis vaccines—Safety regulations—Maine--Bangor	______
10. Separating machinery industry—Corrupt practices—London	______

Chapter 6
FREE FLOATING SUBDIVISIONS AND PATTERN HEADINGS

Free-Floating Subdivisions

The term "free-floating subdivision" refers to form or topical subdivisions that could apply to many subject headings. In the interest of saving space, they are not listed under every heading for which they might be appropriate; instead lists are provided in the *Manual* and in the publication *Free-floating subdivisions: an alphabetical index*. The cataloger may assign these subdivisions as required to various subject headings, without specific instructions from within LCSH.

- They may not appear separately in the printed or online version.
- Sometimes they can be found via instructions under the subject heading they represent.
- They must be used in accordance with the guidelines in the *Manual*.
- Not every free-floating subdivision may be used against every heading.

Example

Item A monthly magazine for dentists

The item is about dentistry, so the main topic is **Dentistry**.
The item is also a periodical.

Look at LCSH at the heading **Periodicals**, which provides the instruction
SA *subdivision* Periodicals *under specific subjects, e.g.*
Engineering—Periodicals;
United States—History—Periodicals.

So the subject heading is
Dentistry—Periodicals.

Note that **—Periodicals** is a free-floating subdivision. A complete list of free-floating subdivisions can be found in section H1095 in the *Manual*, along with instructions about their use. The list has been reproduced at the back of this book.

EXERCISE 6.1

Are the following subject headings and subdivisions correctly established? If not, why not?

Headings	Correct/ Incorrect	Reason and correct form (if incorrect)
1. Dentistry—Law and legislation		
2. Paper industry—History		
3. Buildings—Maintenance		
4. Buildings—Maintenance and repair		
5. Books—Reviews—Periodicals		
6. Dentistry—Book reviews		
7. Real property—Finance, personal		
8. Chicago (Ill.)—Appropriations and expenditure		

EXERCISE 6.2

Using LCSH, allocate suitable subject headings to the following. Include one or more subdivisions to make your heading more specific.

Topic	Subject heading
1. Bibliography on plant migration	____________________
2. Colonization of Zimbabwe	____________________
3. Pensions of bus drivers in Mexico	____________________
4. History of the laws regulating collection agencies in New Zealand	____________________
5. Satirical cartoons of nurses	____________________
6. Laboratories for sensory evaluation in Geneva	____________________
7. Diagnosis of mouth cancer in Glasgow	____________________
8. Testing of instruments used in nuclear power plants in Tokyo	____________________
9. Deterioration of murals in Venice	____________________
10. Chinese coiffures in the 18th century	____________________

Pattern Headings

Introduction

Standardized sets of topical and form subdivisions have been developed for use under particular categories of subject headings or name headings. To avoid repeating these subdivisions under all possible subject headings, only one or a few representative headings from each category are printed in LCSH. These headings form patterns for other headings in their category. In this way they are a form of free-floating subdivision. The general free-floating subdivisions may not be included in all pattern headings.

You should consult the *Manual* for the lists of free-floating subdivisions controlled by pattern headings (H 1147-H 1200) and other free-floating subdivisions if needed. Extracts from this section of the manual can be found at the back of this book.

Subdivisions authorized for free-floating use have not generally been included in the lists of free-floating subdivisions controlled by pattern headings. It is frequently necessary to consult H 1095, H 1100, the list of free-floating subdivisions used under classes of persons and H 1105, the list of free-floating sub-divisions used under corporate bodies, in addition to a specific pattern heading list when constructing subject headings with free-floating subdivisions.

Pattern headings have not been designated for all possible categories in the world of knowledge. Not all headings in the LCSH system are covered by pattern headings.

General Rule

Use any subdivision that is established under a pattern heading as a free-floating subdivision with any other heading belonging to its category, if it is appropriate and if no conflicting heading is established in the subject authority file.

Procedure

1. Find the correct form of the main heading.
2. Check LCSH under the subject heading for the desired subdivision. If found, stop here.
3. If not found, check the list of free-floating subdivisions, or check for a free-floater as a heading.
4. If not found, check the list of Pattern Headings to find an appropriate category. Do not use a heading at the broader level (representing a class of items). You may need to check the list of free-floating subdivisions controlled by pattern headings as well.
5. Note: If two or more pattern headings are designated to represent a category, a subdivision established under any of these headings may be used as free-floating for a heading in that category if it is appropriate.
6. Once the correct pattern heading is located, use any of the subdivisions as required.

Note: subdivisions used as pattern headings are a type of free-floating subdivision. Most of them will appear in the list of free-floating subdivisions at the start of the print version of LCSH. When using this list, it is important to read the scope notes carefully, because the scope note will indicate the type of heading that the subdivision can be used with.

Example:

Title Drought tolerance of rice varieties in Thailand

Procedure

1. **Rice**: But no appropriate subdivision is found
2. No free-floating subdivision is suitable.
3. Look for the category. **Rice** belongs to the category **Plants and crops**. The pattern heading for this category is **Corn**.
4. Go to **Corn** in LCSH and look for a suitable subdivision. Note all instructions that apply to this heading (e.g., *May Subd Geog)* also apply to the heading you have selected.

Subject heading **Rice —Drought tolerance—Thailand**

Pattern Headings Listed in Subject Cataloging Manual

Subdivisions Controlled by Pattern Headings H 1146

List of pattern headings. Below and on the following pages is a chart showing pattern headings established to date. They are arranged first by major discipline, then by special category.

Subject Field	*Category*	*Pattern Heading(s)*	
THE ARTS	Art	Art, Italian Art, Chinese Art, Japanese Art, Korean	H 1148
	Groups of literary authors (including authors, poets, dramatists, etc.)	Authors, English	H 1155.2
	Literary works entered under author	Shakespeare, William, 1564-1616. Hamlet	H 1155.6
	Literary works entered under title	Beowulf	H 1155.8
	Languages and groups of languages	English language French language Romance languages	H 1154
	Literatures (including individual genres)	English literature	H 1156
	Music compositions	Operas	H 1160
	Musical instruments	Piano Clarinet	H 1161

Subject Field	*Category*	*Pattern Heading(s)*	
RELIGION	Religious and monastic orders	Jesuits	H 1186
	Religions	Buddhism	H 1185
	Christian denominations	Catholic Church	II 1187
	Sacred works (including parts)	Bible	H 1188

Subject Field	*Category*	*Pattern Heading(s)*	
SCIENCE AND TECHNOLOGY	Land vehicles	Automobiles	H 1195
	Materials	Concrete Metals	H 1158
	Chemicals	Copper Insulin	H 1149
	Organs and regions of the body	Heart Foot	H 1164
	Diseases	Cancer Tuberculosis	H 1150
	Plants and crops	Corn	H 1180
	Animals	Fishes Cattle	H 1147

Subject Field	*Category*	*Pattern Heading(s)*	
HISTORY AND GEOGRAPHY	Colonies of individual countries	Great Britain-Colonies	H 1149.5
	Legislative bodies (including individual chambers)	United States. Congress	H 1155
	Military services (including arrnies, navies, marines, etc.)	United States-Armed Forces United States. Air Force United States. Army United States. Marine Corps United States. Navy	H 1159
	Wars	World War, 1939-1945 United States-History-Civil War, 1861-1865	H 1200

Subject Field	*Category*	*Pattern Heading(s)*	
SOCIAL SCIENCES	Industries	Construction industry	H 1153
		Retail trade	
	Types of educational institutions	Universities and colleges	H 1151.5
	Individual educational institutions	Harvard University	H 1151
	Legal topics	Labor laws and legislation	H 1154.5

Exercise 6.3

Using LCSH, find appropriate subject headings for the following. Make a note of the pattern heading if used.

Topic	Pattern heading	Heading
1. The lifecycle of the chipmunk	______________	______________
2. Vaccinating cats	______________	______________
3. Ellipsis in Albanian	______________	______________
4. The psychotropic effects of iodine	______________	______________
5. Economic conditions of Dutch colonies in Asia	______________	______________
6. Breeding lions	______________	______________
7. Origins of Zen Buddhism in Japan	______________	______________
8. Anti-lock brake systems for dune buggies	______________	______________
9. How drugs affect the brain	______________	______________
10. Regional variations in the macadamia nut industry (hint: this is an industry)	______________	______________
11. Production standards of films adapted from Arabic children's stories	______________	______________

12. Research on methods of painting of plastics
13. How French has had an impact on English
14. Genetic engineering of sheep in New Zealand
15. How to fix vapor lock problems in buses

EXERCISE 6.4

Are the following subject headings correct? If not, indicate a possible correct heading.

Topic	Subject heading
1. Liver—Size	
2. Canada. Parliament—Duties of members	
3. Spring wheat—Diseases and pests—Italy—Biological control	
4. Sino-French War, 1884-1885—Battles	
5. Guitar—Strings—Materials	
6. Dogs—Embryos—Canada—Transplantation	
7. Llamas—Peru—Handling	
8. Toes, Dislocation of	
9. Ranunculus—Time of flowering	
10. Canola—Disease and pest resistance—Genetic aspects	

Chapter 7
GEOGRAPHIC NAMES AND SUBDIVISIONS

Place names (jurisdictional and non-jurisdictional), including geographic features areas and regions, city sections, early cities, empires, kingdoms, etc. may all be used as name headings in LCSH.

Geographic Names

Geographic names are used in subject cataloging as:

1. Headings
   Australia—Description and travel

2. Subdivisions
   Corn—Iowa

3. Qualifiers
   Corinthian Hall (Kansas City, Mo.)

4. Part of an adjectival or inverted heading
   French drama
   Dramatists, French

Geographic names generally fall into two categories:

- Names for political jurisdictions (e.g., using the name of the geographic area to represent the name of the government)
  i.e., the name as a corporate body, e.g.,
  South Dakota
  Canada
  (In this category are included names of countries, provinces, states, cities and towns)

- Names for areas that are not covered by a political jurisdiction
  i.e., place names, e.g.,
  Australia, Southeastern
  Great Barrier Reef (Qld.)

In this category are included names of natural geographic features
e.g., **Mississippi River**
and built structures
e.g., **Golden Gate Bridge (San Francisco, Calif.)**

Jurisdictional Headings

General Rule

AACR2R Chapter 23 gives the basic principles for establishing these names. *Cataloging service bulletins* of the Library of Congress provide guidance with new names and changes to names.

In brief:

- Use the English form of name if there is one in general use, otherwise the form in the official language of the country (*AACR2R*, 23.2).

- Use only the latest name of a jurisdiction as long as the territorial identity remains essentially unchanged. For example, although both Ceylon and Sri Lanka are valid name headings according to *AACR2R*, only Sri Lanka is used in subject cataloging (*Manual*, H 708).

- For situations where jurisdictions have merged or split, various headings may be appropriate depending on the area and time period discussed. In general, assign subject headings that correspond to the physical extent of the area being discussed.

- If additions are required to place names, use parentheses.

Identifying between Identical Place Names

- Add a word or phrase commonly used to distinguish them, e.g.,
  Tarbert (Strathclyde, Scotland)
  Tarbert (Western Isles, Scotland)

  If necessary to identify the place (as in the case of a community within a city), give the name of an appropriate smaller place before the name of the specified larger place, e.g.,
  Hyde Park (Chicago, Ill.)
  Chelsea (London, England)

- If the first part of a place name is a term indicating a type of jurisdiction, and the place is commonly listed under another element of its name in lists published in the language of the country in which it is located, omit the term indicating the type of jurisdiction.
  Kerry (Ireland)
  not
  County Kerry (Ireland)

- In all other cases, include the jurisdictional term, e.g.,
  District of Colombia (Mexico City, Mexico)

Non-Jurisdictional Headings

A range of entities can be established as headings. These include:

- Ancient cities
- Archaeological sites, historic sites, etc
- Areas and regions (when not free-floating)
- Boundary lines
- Bridges
- Canals
- City sections
- Dams
- Farms, ranches, gardens
- Forests, grasslands, etc.
- Geologic basins, geologic formations, etc.
- Mines
- Parks, reserves, refuges, recreation areas, etc.
- Reservoirs
- Roads, streets, trails
- Tunnels

and geographic features including

basins	gorges	plateaus
bays	gulfs	rivers
canyons	lagoons	seas
capes	lakes	sounds
caves	moors	steppes
creeks	mountains	straits
deserts	ocean currents	tonal islands
falls	peninsulas	
fjords	plains	

Geographic Headings That Are Qualified (H 810)

Geographic qualifiers are additions to a place name, enclosed in parentheses, indicating the broader jurisdiction in which the place is located. Most places used as subject headings are qualified (rare exceptions being geographic features that span a number of jurisdictions, e.g., river systems). Always qualify by the name of the jurisdiction **except for the following countries:**

Australia	use names of states
Canada	use names of provinces
Great Britain	use names of constituent countries
United States	use names of states
Malaysia	use names of states
Serbia and Montenegro	use names of republics

For a full list of the political divisions for these six exceptions, and the forms to be used as qualifiers, see the *Subject cataloging manual H 810.*

EXERCISE 7.1

Using LCSH, establish the following geographic features as headings:

Topic	Subject heading
1. Kythnos Island	
2. Isle Royale National Park	
3. Royal National Park (south of Sydney)	
4. Central Park (in New York)	
5. Statue of Liberty	
6. Grand Canyon	
7. Aaron Webster Cemetery (in Michigan)	
8. Merri River	
9. London River (in France)	
10. Amazon River	
11. Death Valley	
12. Bond Street (London)	
13. 17th Street in Washington	
14. Highway 40 (United States)	
15. Hilo Bay	
16. Brooklyn Bridge (in New York)	
17. Ayers Rock National Park	
18. Mount Whitney in California	
19. The Vatican	
20. Wailing Wall (in Jerusalem)	

Direct Geographic Subdivisions

General Rule

If a geographic subdivision is at the country level or above, the name of the place follows the main heading or subdivision at the instruction *(May Subd Geog)*

e.g., Futurism (Art)—France
Health occupations students—Mexico
Geology—Antarctica.

In addition, first order political divisions in

Canada	provinces
United States	states
Great Britain	constituent countries (i.e., England, Wales, Scotland, Northern Ireland)

also follow the topical element directly.

So we have
Health occupations students—British Columbia
Railroads—Scotland
Geology—Australia--New South Wales

Indirect Geographic Subdivisions

General Rule

In many cases, the name of a larger geographic entity is placed before the name of a more specific locality. This is described as assigning the place name *indirectly.* Places below national level are normally assigned indirectly.

Generally, the name of the country is interposed between the topic and the subordinate political or geographic division.

e.g., Labor supply—France—Paris
instead of
Labor supply—Paris

Litter (Trash)—Italy—Venice
instead of
Litter (Trash)—Venice

Narcotic clinics—Thailand—Bangkok
instead of
Narcotic clinics—Bangkok

Exception

For places in Canada, the United States and Great Britain, interpose the name of the first-order political division between the topic and the subordinate political or geographic division.

e.g., Labor supply—California—Los Angeles
not
Labor supply—United States—Los Angeles

Narcotic clinics—Scotland—Glasgow
not
Narcotic clinics—Great Britain—Glasgow

As a general rule, the geographic subdivision follows the last element that can be divided by place (that is, which contains the designation *(May Subd Geog)*).

e.g., Construction industry *(May Subd Geog)*
—Finance
——Law and legislation *(May Subd Geog))*
—Government policy *(May Subd Geog)*
—Inventories

So the heading for a work on law and legislation in the construction industry in Indonesia is
Construction industry—Finance—Law and legislation—Indonesia

EXERCISE 7.2

Using LCSH, allocate suitable subject headings to the following. Include one or more subdivisions to make your heading more specific.

Topic	Subject heading
1. Diseases of the eyelids in China	____________________
2. Diseases of the limbs in Africa	____________________
3. Taxation of show business personalities in Australia	____________________
4. The labeling of bread in Houston	____________________
5. The legislation on bread labelling in Oregon	____________________

6. Abnormalities of cattle in Argentina ______________________

7. Collective agreements in the airlines in Belgium ______________________

8. Job stress in health professionals in Virginia ______________________

9. A report on potato pests in Victoria (a state in Australia) ______________________

10. Historical monuments in Mankato, Minnesota ______________________

EXERCISE 7.3

Using LCSH, provide subject headings for the following titles (topics), including geographic subdivisions.

Topic	Subject heading
1. American libraries	______________________
2. Hospitals in Albuquerque	______________________
3. A field guide to birds around Billings in Montana	______________________
4. Laws regulating online gambling in southeast Asia	______________________
5. A report on the police in Utah	______________________
6. Body surfing on the Gold Coast	______________________
7. Black colleges in the United States	______________________
8. Australian badgers (Vombatidae) of the south-eastern region of Australia	______________________
9. Art colonies in Tucson	______________________
10. Traditional Spanish folk beliefs	______________________

11. Painters from Rocksprings, Wyoming ______________________

12. Research into the climate of Anchorage ______________________

13. Bridges in Rome ______________________

14. Walking in Richmond, Virginia ______________________

15. Education in Vermont ______________________

Chapter 8
NAMES

The following types of names can be used as subject headings:

- **personal names**, including names of legendary, mythological and fictitious characters, gods etc.
- **family names**, including dynasties and royal houses
- **place names** (jurisdictional and nonjurisdictional), including geographic features areas and regions, city sections, early cities, empires, kingdoms, etc.
- **names of corporate bodies**
- **names of art works**
- **names of chemicals, drugs and minerals**
- **biological names**
- other names, e.g., languages (including computer languages), ethnic groups, roads, structures, buildings, railroads, projects, movements, events, trade names, games.

Note: LCSH includes personal names, names of corporate bodies, jurisdictional names, and uniform titles only if they require special treatment.

It is always useful to check names in an authority file. Authority files are treated in Chapter 9.

Personal Names

Biography (H 1330)

The biography or autobiography of a person requires the use of a personal name subject heading.

Biography refers to the genre of works consisting of the life histories of individuals, whether written by the individual themselves or by others.

Individual biography refers to a work about the life of one individual.

Collective biography refers to a work about the lives of two or more persons.

A complete biography is a work about the life span of one person.

A partial biography gives only some details about a person's life.

In order to be considered a biography, a work should present personal details of the biographee, in at least 50% of the available space. Personal details of birth, education, marriage, personal habits and experiences, death and so on should be synthesised and presented as a whole.

Biographical Subdivisions

There are a number of subdivisions that can be used to bring out different aspects of a person's life or work.

- Subdivisions under pattern headings can be used:

    The pattern heading category **Individual literary authors** was discontinued in 1998. Instead, any appropriate free-floating subdivisions under names of persons (H 1110) may be applied.

    For subdivisions under literary works entered under author, use the pattern heading for:
    Shakespeare, William, 1564-1616. Hamlet

    For subdivisions under literary works entered under title, use the pattern for:
    Beowulf

- Form subdivisions that designate biography
    The subdivision **—Biography** designates individual and collective biography, autobiography, personal reminiscences and personal narratives.

General Rules

- Assign to any biographical work, whether individual or collective, a combination of the following types of headings :
    - [name or names of persons discussed]
    - [class of persons to which the persons discussed belong] **—Biography**
    - [additional biographical headings for organization, ethnic group, place, event, gender]
    - [additional specific topics, as appropriate]

- Do not subdivide the name heading for a person by the subdivision **—Biography**. Simply use the correct form of the personal name as the subject heading.

- Bring out the names of persons discussed (usually only 3-4). If a collective biography discusses more than 3-4 persons, do not allocate individual name subject headings.

- Use the personal name for a head of state or other official, not the corporate head of state heading.

- Use subdivisions from the free-floating subdivisions or pattern headings lists.

- Bring out the subject area or activity that the person is associated with
    - [class of person]—[place]—Biography

    e.g., **Plumbers—Maryland—Biography**

- Allocate additional biographical headings where possible to bring out any of the following:
    - organization
    - ethnic group
    - place
    - event
    - gender

Partial Biography

If the work treats the life of an individual as one aspect of a fuller treatment, look for personal biographical details of approximately 20%, even if the complete life history is not included. If the personal biography of 20% is not present, still include the name of the person but do not allocate biographical headings

e.g.,		
	Title	The personal life of a general during a war
	Subject headings	1. Patton, George S. (George Smith), 1885-1945 2. World War, 1939-1945—Biography 3. Generals—United States—Biography 4. United States. Army—Biography

EXERCISE 8.1

Using an authority file, provide a subject heading for each of the following:

Topic	Subject heading
1. Shakespeare	______________________
2. Antonia Byatt	______________________
3. T.S. Eliot	______________________
4. Joan of Arc	______________________
5. Queen Elizabeth II	______________________
6. The Tower of London	______________________
7. Empire State Building	______________________
8. Agustus Agar	______________________
9. The Tyree Family	______________________
10. Immanuel Kant	______________________

EXERCISE 8.2

Using LCSH, provide appropriate subject headings including subdivisions for the following. You may need to check an authority file for the verified forms of names.

Topic	Subject heading
1. Biography of Earl Warren, a governor of California	____________________
2. Biography of Tony Bennett	____________________
3. A collective biography of the last 10 Presidents of the United States and the events that took place during their tenure	____________________
4. The history of the Pulitzer Prize	____________________
5. The family history of the Taylor family	____________________

Chapter 9
SUBJECT AUTHORITY FILES

Introduction

Authority control is the maintenance of standard forms of headings in the catalog, so that library users can locate information using consistent subject, name and title headings. It also ensures that all future additions to the catalog use the same heading as an access point.

An **authority file** is the record of the correct form of names, series, subjects or uniform titles used in a catalog. It represents a record of decisions made by the cataloger in accordance with the library's policy. It records the standard form of a heading, as prescribed by *AACR2R,* and all references made to and from the headings.

The largest authority file is *Library of Congress Authorities (LCA)* which is available online at authorities.loc.gov. It is searchable by subject, name, title and name/title.

A **subject authority file** is a file of all the subject headings used in the catalog. It also contains references made to the headings. This controls the library's use of subject headings and ensures collocation of records that have the same access point.

An **authority record** is a separate record for each heading. It contains the correct form of the heading, references and notes relating to the reference source used to verify the name.

Two sorts of headings appear in a subject authority file:

- authorized headings/preferred terms that appear in the catalog only
- unauthorized headings/non-preferred terms with a USE reference to the preferred term.

Catalogers normally

1. check for headings used in their catalog
2. if the heading is not found, check an external authority file (e.g., LCA or Canadian Subject Headings)
3. if not found, check the subject list (e.g., LCSH) and construct the required heading
4. perform authority work to include the new heading and any references or links to other headings in the authority file.

A Manual Subject Authority Record

Subject Heading
Scope note

UF	**Used For :** Non-preferred terms from which Use references will be made to the heading at the top of the card
BT	**Broader Term :** Subject headings from which *see also* references will be made to the heading at the top of the card
RT	**Related Term :** Subject headings to and from which *see also* references will be made to and from the heading at the top of the card
NT	**Narrower Term :** Subject headings to which a *see also* reference will be made from the subject heading at the top of the card
SA	**See Also :** General *see also* reference

Reference source

An Online Subject Authority Record

AUTHORITY DISPLAY

va voc00-23007 db 07/16/80 12/08/89 ---- ----

CSIRO

UF C.S.I.R.O.
UF Commonwealth Scientific and Industrial Research Organisation (Australia)
UF Commonwealth Scientific and Industrial Research Organization (Australia)

Former name
Council for Scientific and Industrial Research (Australia)

Scope
In 1949 the Council for Scientific and Industrial Research (CSIR) changes its name to the Commonwealth Scientific and Industrial Research Organization (CSIRO). In 1986 the CSIRO changes the spelling of its name, with the word 'Organization' becoming 'Organization'. Works by these bodies are found under the name used at the time of publication.

Procedures for Creating a Subject Authority Record

The following procedures for establishing a subject authority record take you through all the types of references used in an online subject authority file, with the associated MARC coding. Bear in mind that you may not have to use all the references in the subject headings list. Libraries vary in the extent to which references are made, and the cataloger should always bear in mind the library's cataloging policy.

The procedures are demonstrated using the following example.

Enemy property
Here are entered works on the treatment of enemy property taken on land. Works on enemy property taken at sea are entered under Capture at sea.

UF	Captured property
BT	Confiscations
RT	Alien property
	Requisitions, Military
	Trading with the enemy
SA	*subdivision* Confiscations and contributions *under individual wars, e.g.* World War, 1939-1945—Confiscations and contributions
NT	Booty (International law)
	Military occupation damages

1. Code the subject heading.

150	0	$aEnemy property

2. Include any necessary scope notes.

150	0	$aEnemy property
680		$iHere are entered works on the treatment of enemy property taken on land. Works on enemy property taken at sea are entered under$aCapture at sea
681		$iNote under$aCapture at sea

3. Then add any general (SA) references

150	0	$aEnemy property
360		$isubdivision$aConfiscations and contributions$iunder individual wars, e.g. $aWorld War, 1939-1945—Confiscations and contributions
680		$iHere are entered works on the treatment of enemy property taken on land. Works on enemy property taken at sea are entered under$aCapture at sea
681		$iNote under$aCapture at sea

4. Then add any “seen from” (Used For) references.

```
150 0   $aEnemy property
360     $isubdivision$aConfiscations and contributions$iunder individual wars,
        e.g. $aWorld War, 1939-1945—Confiscations and contributions
450 0   $aCaptured property
680     $iHere are entered works on the treatment of enemy property taken on
        land. Works on enemy property taken at sea are entered under$aCapture
        at sea
681     $iNote under$aCapture at sea
```

5. Then add any “seen also from” references. Note that the code “g” in subfield “w” indicates a Broader Term relationship.

```
150 0   $aEnemy property
360     $isubdivision$aConfiscations and contributions$iunder individual wars,
        e.g. $aWorld War, 1939-1945—Confiscations and contributions
450 0   $aCaptured property
550 0   $wg$aConfiscations
680     $iHere are entered works on the treatment of enemy property taken on
        land. Works on enemy property taken at sea are entered under$aCapture
        at sea
681     $iNote under$aCapture at sea
```

6. Add related terms if you need them.

```
150 0   $aEnemy property
450 0   $aCaptured property
550 0   $wg$aConfiscations
550 0   $aAlien property
550 0   $aRequisitions, Military
550 0   $aTrading with the enemy
```

7. Finally, include a reference(s) to a narrower term(s). Code “h” in subfield “w” indicates the Narrower Term relationship.

```
150 0   $aEnemy property
450 0   $aCaptured property
550 0   $wg$aConfiscations
550 0   $aAlien property
550 0   $aRequisitions, Military
550 0   $aTrading with the enemy
550 0   $wh$aBooty (International law)
550 0   $wh$aMilitary occupational damages
```

The final record is:

150	0	$aEnemy property
360		$isubdivision$aConfiscations and contributions$iunder individual wars, e.g. $aWorld War, 1939-1945—Confiscations and contributions
450	0	$aCaptured property
550	0	wgaConfiscations
550	0	$aAlien property
550	0	$aRequisitions, Military
550	0	$aTrading with the enemy
550	0	whaBooty (International law)
550	0	whaMilitary occupational damages
680		$iHere are entered works on the treatment of enemy property taken on land. Works on enemy property taken at sea are entered under$aCapture at sea
681		$iNote under$aCapture at sea

8. Depending on your online system, you may have to go into each of the headings referred to, in order to establish the corresponding reciprocal references.

150	0	$aConfiscations
550	0	whaBooty (International law)
550	0	whaEnemy property
550	0	whaMonetary gold confiscation
550	0	whaRefugee property
550	0	whaRequisitions, Military

150	0	$aAlien property
450	0	$aAssets, Foreign
450	0	$aProperty, alien
550	0	wgaAliens
550	0	wgaInternational law
550	0	$aEnemy property
550	0	whaAmerican property
550	0	whaAustrian property
550	0	whaBelgian property
		(and so on, as well as for other related terms)

150	0	$aBooty (International law)
450	0	$aCaptured property
550	0	wgaConfiscations
550	0	wgaEnemy property
550	0	wgaMilitary occupation
550	0	wgaPrizes
550	0	wgaSearches and seizures
		(and so on, as well as for other narrower terms)

References in the Catalog

In online catalogs, the display of references varies considerably. The corresponding catalog references for the headings above may look like this:

Enemy property
Here are entered works on the treatment of enemy property taken on land. Works on enemy property taken at sea are entered under
Capture at sea

See also Alien property
Requisitions, Military
Trading with the enemy

Captured property

SEE Enemy property

Alien property

See also Enemy property

Requisitions, Military

See also Enemy property

Trading with the enemy

See also Enemy property

EXERCISE 9.1

Using *LCSH*, create the necessary subject authority record for the heading **Work**, and indicate what changes need to be made to existing records.

Work

Here are entered works on the physical or mental exertion of individuals to produce or accomplish something. Works on the collective human activities involved in the production and distribution of goods and services are entered under Labor.

UF Industry (Psychology)
Method of work
Work, method of
BT Human behavior
RT Labor
Occupations
NT Division of labor
Hours of labor
Labor time
...

Chapter 10
MORE PRACTICE

EXERCISE 10.1

Using LCSH, find subject headings, with subdivisions where appropriate, and code using MARC 21.

	Topic	Subject heading
1.	AACRII - a computer-based training package	________________
2.	Adopted children : a new look at their civil rights	________________
3.	The anti-vivisection movement : a history	________________
4.	The art of growing daffodils	________________
5.	The artists of Spain : works on exhibition	________________
6.	Business English : how to write business letters	________________
7.	Car pools in San Francisco	________________
8.	Carrying out public relations for the Library of Congress	________________
9.	Adolescent health services in Denmark	________________
10.	Collected biographies of Mexican musicians	________________
11.	Constitutional law in Massachusetts	________________
12.	Cooking Egyptian cuisine	________________
13.	Cooking in Egypt	________________
14.	Diagnosing brain abscesses	________________
15.	A bibliography of education for librarianship	________________

EXERCISE 10.2

	Topic	Subject heading
1.	The effects of pollution on rice-growing	__________
2.	Electric power development	__________
3.	Encyclopaedia of the Aztecs	__________
4.	Eroticism in art	__________
5.	Personal stories of American soldiers in the Korean War	__________
6.	Biological treatment of sewage	__________
7.	Grist for the mill : the flour mills of Brazil	__________
8.	Hallelujah I'm a bum : a study of tramps and hoboes	__________
9.	Harrap German-Spanish-German dictionary	__________
10.	A history of the People's Republic of China from 1950-1975	__________
11.	House plans by architects	__________
12.	How real is telekinesis?	__________
13.	How to tune a French horn	__________
14.	How to tune a piano	__________
15.	An introduction to Eskimo folksongs	__________

EXERCISE 10.3

	Topic	Subject heading
1.	Medieval history	______________
2.	Telephone directory of Columbus, Nebraska	______________
3.	Mendicants : a history of begging	______________
4.	The model ship catalog	______________
5.	Negotiation in the hostage situation	______________
6.	A new bibliography of fiction about dogs	______________
7.	The dating of porcelain from China	______________
8.	The psychological effects of being unemployed	______________
9.	Relations between Judaism and Islam	______________
10.	Rhymes and poetry for children	______________
11.	Corrosion of iron and concrete	______________
12.	The story of the Holy Grail	______________
13.	Snakes of Kentucky	______________
14.	A study of parents without partners	______________
15.	Surfboard riding in Hawaii	______________

EXERCISE 10.4

	Topic	Subject heading
1.	Surgeons in the Argentine Navy (Hint: check a name authority file for the correct form of name)	______________________
2.	Pilot Creek in Texas	______________________
3.	Public access to the Internet in libraries	______________________
4.	Techniques for photographing birds	______________________
5.	A collection of photographs of the Vietnam War (not a book of reproduced photos)	______________________
6.	Television repair manual	______________________
7.	Public library services to preschoolers	______________________
8.	Easy dried flower pictures	______________________
9.	Measuring the earth's gravitational pull	______________________
10.	The five commandments of Buddhism	______________________
11.	Judging English riding	______________________
12.	Transportation of nuclear wastes : legal requirements in Germany	______________________
13.	Ice-climbing in Nepal	______________________
14.	When your partner dies	______________________
15.	Reusing your wastepaper	______________________

MARC CODES

The *MARC 21 concise format for bibliographic data* is available on the Internet at www.loc.gov/marc/bibliographic/ecbdhome.html

600 SUBJECT ADDED ENTRY - PERSONAL NAME (R)

A subject added entry in which the entry element is a personal name.

Indicators
First Type of personal name entry element
0 Forename
1 Surname
3 Family name
Second Subject heading system/thesaurus
0 Library of Congress Subject Headings/LC authority files
1 LC subject headings for children's literature
2 Medical Subject Headings/NLM authority files
3 National Agricultural Library subject authority file
4 Source not specified
5 Canadian Subject Headings/LAC authority file
6 Repertoire des vedettes-matiere/LAC authority file

Subfield Codes
$a Personal name (NR)
$b Numeration (NR)
$c Titles and other words associated with a name (R)
$d Dates associated with a name (NR)
$e Relator term (R)
$f Date of a work (NR)
$g Miscellaneous information (NR)
$h Medium (NR)
$k Form subheading (R)
$l Language of a work (NR)
$n Number of part/section of a work (R)
$p Name of part/section of a work (R)
$q Fuller form of name (NR)
$s Version (NR)
$t Title of a work (NR)
$v Form subdivision (R)
$x General subdivision (R)
$y Chronological subdivision (R)
$z Geographic subdivision (R)

Examples
600 00 $aNorodom Sihanouk,$cPrince,$d1922-
600 30 $aDunlop family.
600 10 $aDrake, Francis,$cSir,$d1540?-1596.
600 10 $aShakespeare, William,$d1564-1616.$tHamlet.

600 10 $aShakespeare, William,$d1564-1616$xCriticism and interpretation$xHistory$y18th century.
600 10 $aPushkin, Aleksandr Sergeevich,$d1799-1837$xMuseums, relics, etc.$zRussia (Federation)$zMoscow$vMaps.
600 10 $aNixon, Richard M.$q(Richard Milhouse),$d1913-1994$xPersonality.

610 SUBJECT ADDED ENTRY - CORPORATE NAME (R)

A subject added entry in which the entry element is a corporate name.

Indicators
First Type of corporate name entry element
- 0 Inverted name
- 1 Jurisdiction name
- 2 Name in direct order

Second Thesaurus
- 0 Library of Congress Subject Headings/LC authority files
- 1 LC subject headings for children's literature
- 2 Medical Subject Headings/NLM authority files
- 3 National Agricultural Library subject authority file
- 4 Source not specified
- 5 Canadian Subject Headings/LAC authority file
- 6 Repertoire des vedettes-matiere/LAC authority file

Subfield Codes
- $a Corporate name or jurisdiction name as entry element (NR)
- $b Subordinate unit (R)
- $c Location of meeting (NR)
- $d Date of meeting or treaty signing (R)
- $e Relator term (R)
- $f Date of a work (NR)
- $g Miscellaneous information (NR)
- $h Medium (NR)
- $k Form subheading (R)
- $l Language of a work (NR)
- $n Number of part/section/meeting (R)
- $p Name of part/section of a work (R)
- $r Key for music (NR)
- $s Version (NR)
- $t Title of a work (NR)
- $v Form subdivision (R)
- $x General subdivision (R)
- $y Chronological subdivision (R)
- $z Geographic subdivision (R)

Examples
610 20 $aEmpire State Building (New York, N.Y.)
610 10 $aGreat Britain.$tTreaties, etc.$gIreland,$d1985 Nov. 15.
610 20 $aBritish Library.$kManuscript.$nArundel 384.
610 10 $aUnited States.$bArmy.$bCavalry$xHistory$yCivil War, 1861-1865$vMaps.
610 20 $aUnited Nations$zAfrica.

611 SUBJECT ADDED ENTRY - MEETING NAME (R)

A subject added entry in which the entry element is a meeting name.

Indicators
First Type of meeting name entry element
0 Inverted name
1 Jurisdiction name
2 Name in direct order
Second Thesaurus
0 Library of Congress Subject Headings/LC authority files
1 LC subject headings for children's literature
2 Medical Subject Headings/NLM authority files
3 National Agricultural Library subject authority file
4 Source not specified
5 Canadian Subject Headings/LAC authority file
6 Repertoire des vedettes-matiere/LAC authority file

Subfield Codes
$a Meeting name or jurisdiction name as entry element (NR)
$c Location of meeting (NR)
$d Date of meeting (NR)
$e Subordinate unit (R)
$f Date of a work (NR)
$g Miscellaneous information (NR)
$h Medium (NR)
$k Form subheading (R)
$l Language of a work (NR)
$n Number of part/section/meeting (R)
$p Name of part/section of a work (R)
$s Version (NR)
$t Title of a work (NR)
$v Form subdivision (R)
$x General subdivision (R)
$y Chronological subdivision (R)
$z Geographic subdivision (R)

Examples
611 20 $aVatican Council $n(2nd : $d1962-1965). $tDecretum de presbyterorum ministerio et vita.
611 20 $aWorld Series (Baseball)$xHistory.
611 20 $aOlympic Games $n(23rd : $d1984 : $cLos Angeles, Calif.)$vPeriodicals.

650 SUBJECT ADDED ENTRY - TOPICAL TERM (R)

A subject added entry in which the entry element is a topical term.

Indicators
First Level of subject
- # No information provided
- 0 No level specified
- 1 Primary
- 2 Secondary

Second Subject heading system/thesaurus
- 0 Library of Congress Subject Headings/LC authority files
- 1 LC subject headings for children's literature
- 2 Medical Subject Headings/NLM authority files
- 3 National Agricultural Library subject authority file
- 4 Source not specified
- 5 Canadian Subject Headings/LAC authority file
- 6 Repertoire des vedettes-matiere/LAC authority file
- 7 Source specified in subfield $2

Subfield Codes
- $a Topical term or geographic name as entry element (NR)
- $b Topical term following geographic name as entry element (NR)
- $c Location of event (NR)
- $d Active dates (NR)
- $e Relator term (NR)
- $v Form subdivision (R)
- $x General subdivision (R)
- $y Chronological subdivision (R)
- $z Geographic subdivision (R)

Examples
650 #0 $aArchitecture, Modern$y19th century.
650 00 $aFlour and feed trade$vPeriodicals.
650 #0 $aVocal music$zFrance$y18th century.

651 SUBJECT ADDED ENTRY - GEOGRAPHIC NAME (R)

A subject added entry in which the entry element is a geographic name.

Indicators
First Undefined; contains a blank (#)
Second Thesaurus
- 0 Library of Congress Subject Headings/LC authority files
- 1 LC subject headings for children's literature
- 2 Medical Subject Headings/NLM authority files
- 3 National Agricultural Library subject authority file
- 4 Source not specified
- 5 Canadian Subject Headings/LAC authority file
- 6 Repertoire des vedettes-matiere/LAC authority file

Subfield Codes
$a Geographic name (NR)
$v Form subdivision (R)
$x General subdivision (R)
$y Chronological subdivision (R)
$z Geographic subdivision (R)

Examples
651 #0 $aAmazon River.
651 #0 $aPompeii (Ancient city)
651 #0 $aRussia$xHistory$vMaps.
651 #0 $aUnited States$xBoundaries$zCanada.

ANSWERS

Note: These answers have been verified in the 28th edition of LCSH and the *Subject cataloging manual online (December 2006)*. Some answers may vary according to the editions and updates you are using.

EXERCISE 1.1

1. Subject: the theme of a work

   Subject heading: a term (word or phrase) that represents the theme of a work

2. There are any number, including:

   Library of Congress Subject Headings

   Sears List of Subject Headings

   MeSH: Medical Subject Headings

   SCIS Subject Headings List

   APAIS Thesaurus

EXERCISE 1.2

1. Cataloger:

   - Uses headings in subject cataloging
   - Consistency maintained within catalog

2. Reference advisor:

   - Uses to construct searches when searching the catalog

3. Library user:

   - To construct searches in the catalog

4. Acquisitions officer:

   - Uses headings to identify subject areas a library might collect in
   - Able to search a number of sources for items

5. Interlibrary loans officer:

   - Uses to help find/verify items for loan

6. Author:

   - Helps author to use standard or preferred terminology

EXERCISE 1.3

1. Controlled vocabulary:

    Many library catalogs use LCSH, SCIS

    APAIS and Medline use thesauri

    Uncontrolled vocabulary:

    Full-text databases

    Keyword title search

2. Controlled vocabulary

    Advantages
    - only one term per concept
    - records hierarchical and associative relations of a concept
    - establishes scope of each topic
    - increases probability that the same term will be used by different catalogs
    - speeds retrieval

    Disadvantages
    - highly structured
    - may be cumbersome to use
    - user must "learn" the language

    Uncontrolled vocabulary

    Advantages
    - effort and cost of indexing are reduced
    - process can be automated
    - user can use terms and synonyms requiring no additional knowledge

    Disadvantages
    - can reduce retrieved list if all synonyms are used
    - may retrieve false hits - e.g., with homonyms

EXERCISE 1.4

1. A synonym is a word that has the same meaning as another.

2. Tools include dictionaries, thesauri.

3.

1.	author	writer
2.	stamp collecting	philately
3.	car	automobile, motor car
4.	monograph	book
5.	trailer	campervan
6.	serial	journal, periodical

7.	hiking	tramping
8.	saturated	soaked
9.	slack	loose, careless
10.	corpulence	bulkiness, obesity
11.	elevators	lifts
12.	hirsute	hairy
13.	shore	beach
14.	rage	anger
15.	hemp	marijuana

EXERCISE 1.5

1. A homonym is a word that sounds the same as another, but has a different meaning.

2. Tools include dictionaries.

3.

1. slack	1.	loose
	2.	careless
2. slam	1.	shut with force and noise
	2.	win all tricks (cards) in one deal
3. toast	1.	bread in slices browned on both sides by heat
	2.	words of congratulations or appreciation spoken before drinking
4. lag	1.	fall behind
	2.	cover pipes
5. cuff	1.	trimming on a sleeve
	2.	to strike with open hand

EXERCISE 1.6

1. d. contain useful or important information

2. c. not eating properly and not getting enough exercise
   b. bad features of living in towns
   c. make resolutions to lead a healthier life
   b. it is better to become a Buddhist
   a. their way of life involved both exercise and relaxation

Keywords - fitness, relaxation, yoga

Because of our unhealthy lifestyle, we need to learn to relax, and yoga and exercise can help.

Exercise 2.1

1. Beverage industry
   Beverage processing plants

2. Beverage industry – Employees
   Beverage industry – Employees – Labor unions
   Beverage industry – Equipment and supplies
   Beverage processing plants – Equipment and supplies

3. Beverage industry – United States
   Beverage industry – United States – Employees
   Beverage industry – Employees – Labor unions – United States
   Beverage industry – United States – Equipment and supplies
   Beverage processing plants – United States
   Beverage processing plants – Equipment and supplies

Exercise 2.2

1. **Craftsmen** is not used. **Artisans** is the preferred term which is used.
2. **Apprentices** is narrower than **Artisans**.
3. **Skilled labor** is broader than **Artisans**.
4. **Artisans** and **Cottage industries** are related terms. Both are used.
5. No.

Exercise 2.3

	Subject heading	Correct heading
1.	Felix the Cat	Felix the Cat (Fictitious character)
2.	Guitar—Construction	Correct
3.	Fusion reactors—Fuels	Thermonuclear fuels
4.	Fusion reactors—Germany	Fusion reactors
5.	Semi-conductors	Semiconductors
6.	Guitar and harp music	Correct
7.	Heliophobus plants	Shade-tolerant plants
8.	Seychelles—Coup d'etat, 1977	Seychelles—History—Coup d'etat, 1977

9.	Coups d'etat—Seychelles	Correct
10.	Tempo	TEMPO (Computer program language) OR Tempo (Music) OR Tempo (Phonetics)

EXERCISE 3.1

1.	The sea	Ocean
2.	Adoption services	Adoption agencies
3.	Adriatic Islands	Islands of the Adriatic
4.	Children as actors	Child actors
5.	Ways of monitoring fetal heart rate	Fetal heart rate monitoring
		Traffic noise
7.	Oceanic drilling ships in the Atlantic	Deep-sea drilling ships
8.	Catalan political satire	Political satire, Catalan
9.	An introduction to prehistoric agriculture	Agriculture, Prehistoric
10.	The wonders of horseradish	Horse-radish

EXERCISE 3.2

1.	Morris West's slide collections	West, Morris L., 1916- - Slide collections Add the following note: (as per SA note under Slides (Photography)--Private collections
2.	Water conservation and irrigation efficiency	1. Water Conservation 2. Irrigation efficiency
3.	Cartoon-makers	Animators
4.	Electric condensers	Capacitors
5.	Music for organ and flute	Flute and organ music
6.	Sulky racing	Harness racing
7.	Harmony on the keyboard	Keyboard harmony
8.	Prehistoric cartography	Cartography, Prehistoric
9.	The benefits of asparaginic acid	Aspartic acid
10.	Bakery products	Baked products

EXERCISE 5.1

1.	The cost of constructing railroads	Railroads – Design and construction – Costs 650 #0$aRailroads$cDesign and construction$xCosts

2.	Extensions to buildings	Buildings – Additions 650 #0$aBuildings$xAdditions
3.	Synthesis in organic chemistry	Organic compounds – Synthesis 650 #0$aOrganic compounds$xSynthesis
4.	Data processing in credit bureaus	Credit bureaus – Data processing 650 #0$aCredit bureaus$xData processing
5.	The rights and wages of employees in credit unions	1. Credit unions – Employees 650 #0$aCredit unions$xEmployees 2. Wages – Credit unions 650 #0$aWages$xCredit unions 3. Employee rights 650 #0$aEmployee rights
6.	John Brown's raid on Harpers Ferry	Harpers Ferry (W.Va.) – History – John Brown's Raid, 1859 651 #0$aHarpers Ferry (W.Va)$vHistory$yJohn Brown's Raid, 1859
7.	The 1929 depression in Chicago	Depressions – 1929 – Illinois – Chicago 650 #0$aDepressions$y1929$zIllinois$zChicago
8.	The diagnosis of unipolar depression	Depression, mental – Diagnosis 650 #0$aDepression, mental$xDiagnosis
9.	Renaissance engraving	Engraving, Renaissance 650 #0$aEngraving, Renaissance
10.	Hunting with bows and arrows	Bow hunting 650 #0$aBow hunting

EXERCISE 5.2

1.	Religious aspects of animal experiments from the Islamic viewpoint	Animal experimentation—Religious aspects—Islam 650 #0$aAnimal experimentation$xReligious aspects$xIslam
2.	Subject headings for astronomy	Subject headings—Astronomy 650 #0$aSubject headings$xAstronomy
3.	Christian beliefs about salt	Salt—Religious aspects—Christianity 650 #0$aSalt$xReligious aspects$xChristianity
4.	German words and phrases in the English language	English language—Foreign words and phrases—German 650 #0$aEnglish language$xForeign words and phrases$xGerman

5.	Buddhist aspects of codependency	Codependency—Religious aspects—Buddhism 650 #0$aCodependency$xReligious aspects$xBuddhism

EXERCISE 5.3

Banks and banking – Canada

Banks and banking – Canada – Automation

Banks and banking – Canada – Automation – Equipment and supplies

Banks and banking – Canada – Data processing

Banks and banking – Data processing – Contracting out – Canada

Banks and banking – Government ownership – Canada

EXERCISE 5.4

	Topic	Subject heading
1.	Parachutes—Testing—Equipment—Certification— United States	Parachutes—Testing—equipment and supplies—Certification —United States
2.	Scientific apparatus and instruments—Conservation and restoration	Correct
3.	United States—Climate—Measurement	Correct
4.	Birthparents—Identification—Case studies	Correct
5.	Chamber music—Early works to 1800—England	Chamber music—England—Early works to 1800
6.	Murderers—Civil rights—Boston (Mass.)	Murderers—Civil rights—Massachusetts—Boston
7.	Trade-unions—Accounting—Law and Legislation—Michigan	Labor unions—Accounting—Law and Legislation—Michigan
8.	Tuberculosis vaccines—Maine--Bangor	Correct
9.	Tuberculosis vaccines—Safety regulations—Maine--Bangor	Correct
10.	Separating machinery industry—Corrupt practices—London	Separating machinery industry—Corrupt practices—England—London

EXERCISE 6.1

1.	Dentistry—Law and legislation	Incorrect	Dental laws and legislation
2.	Paper industry—History	Correct	
3.	Buildings—Maintenance	Correct	
4.	Buildings—Maintenance and repair	Allowed, but...	Heading using a free-floating subdivision is allowed, but prefer Buildings—Maintenance, which is included in the list
5.	Books—Reviews—Periodicals	Correct	
6.	Dentistry—Book reviews	Correct	
7.	Real property—Finance, personal	Incorrect	**--Finance, personal** is only allowed under names of individual persons, and under classes of persons and ethnic groups. You may use: 1. Real property 2. Finance, personal
8.	Chicago (Ill.)—Appropriations and expenditure	Incorrect	Chicago (Ill.)—Appropriations and expenditures

EXERCISE 6.2

	Topic	Subject heading
1.	Bibliography on plant migration	Plants – Migration – Bibliography 650 #0$aPlants$xMigration$vBibliography
2.	Colonization of Zimbabwe	Zimbabwe – Colonization 651 #0$aZimbabwe$xColonization
3.	Pensions of bus drivers in Mexico	Bus drivers – Pensions – Mexico 650 #0$aBus drivers$xPensions$zMexico
4.	History of the laws regulating collection agencies in New Zealand	Collection agencies – Law and legislation – New Zealand – History 650 #0$aCollection agencies$xLaw and legislation $zNew Zealand$xHistory
5.	Satirical cartoons of nurses	Nurses – Caricatures and cartoons 650 #0$aNurses$vCaricatures and cartoons
6.	Laboratories for sensory evaluation in Geneva	Sensory evaluation—Switzerland—Geneva—Laboratories 650 #0$aSensory evaluation$zSwitzerland $zGeneva$xLaboratories
7.	Diagnosis of mouth cancer in Glasgow	Mouth—Cancer—Diagnosis—Scotland—Glasgow 650 #0$aMouth$xCancer$xDiagnosis$zScotland $zGlasgow

8.	Testing of instruments used in nuclear power plants in Tokyo	Nuclear power plants—Japan—Tokyo —Instruments—Testing 640 #0$aNuclear power plants$zJapan$zTokyo $xInstruments$xTesting
9.	Deterioration of murals in Venice	Mural painting and decoration—Italy—Venice —Deterioration 650 #0$aMural painting and decoration$zItaly $zVenice$xDeterioration
10.	Chinese coiffures in the 18th century	Hairstyles—China—History—18th century 650 #0$aHairstyles$zChina$xHistory$y18th century

EXERCISE 6.3

	Topic	Pattern heading	Heading
1.	The lifecycle of the chipmunk	Fishes	Chipmunks—Life cycles
2.	Vaccinating cats	Cattle	Cats—Vaccination
3.	Ellipsis in Albanian	English language	Albanian language—Ellipsis
4.	The psychotropic effects of iodine	Copper	Iodine—Psychotropic effects
5.	Economic conditions of Dutch colonies in Asia	Great Britain—Colonies	Netherlands—Colonies—Asia—Economic conditions
6.	Breeding lions	Cattle	Lions—Breeding
7.	Origins of Zen Buddhism in Japan	Buddhism	Zen Buddhism—Japan—Origin
8.	Anti-lock brake systems for dune buggies	Automobiles	Dune buggies—Antilock brake systems
9.	How drugs affect the brain	Foot or Heart	Brain—Effect of drugs on
10.	Regional variations in the macadamia nut industry	Retail trade	Macadamia nut industry—Regional disparities
11.	Production standards of films adapted from Arabic children's stories	English literature	Children's stories, Arabic—Film and video adaptations—Production standards
12.	Research on methods of painting of plastics	Metals	Plastics—Painting—Research
13.	How French has had an impact on English	English language	1. French language—Influence on English 2. English language—Foreign elements—French

14.	Genetic engineering of sheep in New Zealand	Cattle	Sheep—Genetic engineering—New Zealand
15.	How to fix vapor lock problems in buses	Automobiles	Buses—Fuel systems—Vapor lock—Repairing

EXERCISE 6.4

	Topic	Subject heading
1.	Liver—Size	Correct
2.	Canada.Parliament—Duties of members	Canada.Parliament—Powers and duties
3.	Spring wheat—Diseases and pests—Italy —Biological Control	Wheat—Diseases and pests—Biological control—Italy
4.	Sino-French War, 1884-1885—Battles	Chinese-French War, 1884-1885—Campaigns
5.	Guitar—Strings—Materials	Guitar strings—Materials
6.	Dogs—Embryos—Canada—Transplantation	Dogs—Embryos—Transplantation—Canada
7.	Llamas—Peru—Handling	Llamas—Handling—Peru
8.	Toes, Dislocation of	Toes—Dislocation
9.	Ranunculus—Time of flowering	Ranunculus—Flowering time
10.	Canola—Disease and pest resistance—Genetic aspects	Correct

EXERCISE 7.1

1.	Kythnos Island	Kythnos Island (Greece)
2.	Isle Royale National Park	Isle Royale National Park (Mich.)
3	Royal National Park (south of Sydney)	Royal National Park (N.S.W.)
4.	Central Park (in New York)	Central Park (New York, N.Y.)
5.	Statue of Liberty	Statue of Liberty (New York, N.Y.)
6.	Grand Canyon	Grand Canyon (Ariz.)
7.	Aaron Webster Cemetery (in Michigan)	Aaron Webster Cemetery (Auburn Hills, Mich.)
8.	Merri River	Merri River (Vic.)
9.	London River (in France)	London River (France and Switzerland)
10.	Amazon River	Amazon River
11.	Death Valley	Death Valley (Calif. and Nev.)
12.	Bond Street (London)	Bond Street (London, England)

13.	17th Street in Washington	Seventeenth Street (Washington, D.C.)
14.	Highway 40 (United States)	United States Highway 40
15.	Hilo Bay	Hilo Bay (Hawaii)
16.	Brooklyn Bridge (in New York)	Brooklyn Bridge (New York, N.Y.)
17.	Ayers Rock National Park	Uluru-Kata Tjuta National Park (N.T.)
18.	Mount Whitney in California	Whitney, Mount (Calif.)
19.	The Vatican	Vatican Palace (Vatican City)
20.	Wailing Wall (in Jerusalem)	Western Wall (Jerusalem)

EXERCISE 7.2

1.	Diseases of the eyelids in China	Eyelids – Diseases – China 650 #0$aEyelids$xDiseases$zChina
2.	Diseases of the limbs in Africa	Extremities (Anatomy) – Diseases – Africa 650 #0$aExtremities (Anatomy)$xDiseases $zAfrica
3.	Taxation of show business personalities in Australia	Entertainers – Taxation – Australia 650 #0$aEntertainers$xTaxation$zAustralia
4.	The labeling of bread in Houston	Bread – Labeling – Texas – Houston 650 #)$aBread$xLabeling$zTexas$zHouston
5.	The legislation on bread labeling in Oregon	Bread – Labeling – Law and legislation – Oregon 650 #0$aBread$xLabeling$xLaw and legislation $zOregon
6.	Abnormalities of cattle in Argentina	Cattle – Abnormalities – Argentina 650 #0$aCattle$xAbnormalities$zArgentina
7.	Collective agreements in the airlines in Belgium	Collective labor agreements – Aeronautics – Belgium 650 #0$aCollective labor agreements $xAeronautics$zBelgium
8.	Job stress in health professionals in Virginia	Medical personnel – Job stress – Virginia 650 #0$aMedical personnel$xJob stress$zVirginia
9.	A report on potato pests in Victoria (a state in Australia)	Potatoes – Diseases and pests – Australia – Victoria 650 #0$aPotatoes$xDiseases and pests$zAustralia$zVictoria
10.	Historical monuments in Mankato, Minnesota	Monuments – Minnesota – Mankato 650 #0$aMonuments$zMinnesota$zMankato

EXERCISE 7.3

1.	American libraries	Libraries – United States 650 #0$aLibraries$zUnited States
2.	Hospitals in Albuquerque	Hospitals – New Mexico – Albuquerque 650 #0$sHospitals$zNew Mexico$zAlbuquerque
3.	A field guide to birds around Billings in Montana	Birds – Montana – Billings – Identification 650 #0$aBirds$zMontana$zBillings$xIdentification
4.	Laws regulating online gambling in southeast Asia	Internet gambling – Law and legislation – Asia, Southeastern 650 #0$aInternet gambling$xLaw and legislation$zAsia, Southeastern
5.	A report on the police in Utah	Police – Utah 650 #0$aPolice$zUtah
6.	Body surfing on the Gold Coast	Surfing – Australia – Gold Coast (Qld.) 650 #0$aSurfing$zAustralia$zGold Coast (Qld.)
7.	Black colleges in the United States	African American universities and colleges 650 #0$aAfrican American universities and colleges
8.	Australian badgers (Vombatidae) of the south-eastern region of Australia	Wombats – Australia, Southeastern 650 #0$aWombats$zAustralia, Southeastern
9.	Art colonies in Tucson	Artist colonies – Arizona – Tucson 650 #0$aArtist colonies$zArizona$zTucson
10.	Traditional Spanish folk beliefs	Folklore – Spain 650 #0$aFolklore$zSpain
11.	Painters from Rocksprings, Wyoming	Painters – Wyoming – Rocksprings 650 #0$aPainters$zWyoming$zRocksprings
12.	Research into the climate of Anchorage	Climatology – Research – Alaska – Anchorage 650 #0$aClimatology$xResearch$zAlaska $zAnchorage
13.	Bridges in Rome	Bridges – Italy – Rome 650 #0$aBridges$zItaly$zRome
14.	Walking in Richmond, Virginia	Walking – Virginia – Richmond 650 #0$aWalking$zVirginia$zRichmond
15.	Education in Vermont	Education – Vermont 650 #0$aEducation$zVermont

EXERCISE 8.1

1.	William Shakespeare	Shakespeare, William, 1564-1616 600 10$aShakespeare, William,$d1564-1616
2.	Antonia Byatt	Byatt, A. S. (Antonia Susan), 1936- 600 10$aByatt, A. S.,$q(Antonia Susan),$d1936-
3.	T.S. Eliot	Eliot, T.S. (Thomas Stearns), 1888-1963 600 10$aEliot, T. S.,$q(Thomas Stearns),$d1888-1963
4.	Joan of Arc	Joan, of Arc, Saint, 1412-1431 600 00$aJoan $cof Arc, Saint,$d1412-1431
5.	Queen Elizabeth II	Elizabeth II, Queen of Great Britain, 1926- 600 00$aElizabeth $bII $cQueen of Great Britain,$d1926-
6.	The Tower of London	Tower of London (London, England) 610 20$aTower of London (London, England)
7.	Empire State Building	Empire State Building (New York, N.Y.) 610 20$aEmpire State Building (New York, N.Y.)
8.	Agustus Agar	Agar, Agustus, 1890-1986 600 10$aAgar, Agustus,$d1890-1986
9.	The Tyree Family	Tyree family 600 30$aTyree family
10.	Immanuel Kant	Kant, Immanuel, 1724-1804 600 10$aKant, Immanuel,$d1724-1804

EXERCISE 8.2

1.	Biography of Earl Warren, a governor of California	Warren, Earl, 1891-1974 600 10$aWarren, Earl,$d1891-1974
2.	Biography of Tony Bennett	Bennett, Tony, 1926- 600 10$aBennett, Tony,$d1926-
3.	A collective biography of the last 10 Presidents of the United States and the events that took place during their tenure	Presidents – United States – Biography 650 #0$aPresidents$zUnited States$vBiography
4.	The history of the Pulitzer Prize	Pulitzer Prizes – History 650 #0$aPulitzer Prizes$xHistory
5.	The family history of the Taylor family	Taylor family 600 30$aTaylor family

EXERCISE 9.1

New records:

150	0	$aWork
450	0	$aIndustry (Psychology)
450	0	$aMethod of work
450	0	$aWork, Method of
550	0	wgaHuman behavior
550	0	$aLabor
550	0	$aOccupations
550	0	whaDivision of labor
550	0	whaHours of labor
550	0	whaLabor time
680	0	$iHere are entered works on the physical or mental exertion of individuals to produce or accomplish something. Works on the collective human activities involved in the production and distribution of goods and services are entered under Labor.

Changes:

150	0	$aHuman behavior
550	0	whaWork

150	0	$aLabor
550	0	$aWork

150	0	$aOccupations
550	0	$aWork

150	0	$aDivision of labor
550	0	wgaWork

150	0	$aHours of labor
550	0	wgaWork

150	0	$aLabor time
550	0	wgaWork

EXERCISE 10.1

1.	AACRII - a computer-based training package	1. Anglo-American cataloguing rules—Computer assisted instruction 630 00$a Anglo-American cataloguing rules$xComputer assisted instruction 2. Descriptive cataloging—Rules 650 #0$aDescriptive cataloging$xRules
2.	Adopted children : a new look at their civil rights	Adopted children—Civil rights 650 #0$aAdopted children$xCivil rights
3.	The anti-vivisection movement : a history	Vivisection—History 650 #0$aVivisection$xHistory
4.	The art of growing daffodils	Daffodils 650 #0$aDaffodils
5.	The artists of Spain : works on exhibition	Artists—Spain 650 #0$aArtists$zSpain
6.	Business English : how to write business letters	English language—Business English 650 #0$aEnglish language$xBusiness English
7.	Car pools in San Francisco	Car pools – California – San Francisco 650 #0$aCar pools$zCalifornia$zSan Francisco
8.	Carrying out public relations for the Library of Congress	Library of Congress – Public relations 610 20$aLibrary of Congress$xPublic relations
9.	Adolescent health services in Denmark	Teenagers—Medical care—Denmark 650 #0$aTeenagers$xMedical care$zDenmark
10.	Collected biographies of Mexican musicians	Musicians – Mexico – Biography 650 #0$aMusicians$zMexico$vBiography
11.	Constitutional law in Massachusetts	Constitutional law – Massachusetts 650 #0$aConstitutional law$zMassachusetts
12.	Cooking Egyptian cuisine	Cookery, Egyptian 650 #0$aCookery, Egyptian
13.	Cooking in Egypt	Cookery—Egypt 650 #0$aCookery$zEgypt
14.	Diagnosing brain abscesses	Brain—Abscess 650 #0$aBrain$xAbscess
15.	A bibliography of education for librarianship	Library education—Bibliography 650 #0$aLibrary education$vBibliography

EXERCISE 10.2

1.	The effects of pollution on rice-growing	Rice—Effect of pollution on 650 #0$aRice$xEffect of pollution on
2.	Electric power development	Electrification 650 #0$aElectrification
3.	Encyclopaedia of the Aztecs	Aztecs—Encyclopedias 650 #0$aAztecs$vEncyclopedias
4.	Eroticism in art	Erotic art 650 #0$aErotic art
5.	Personal stories of American soldiers in the Korean War	Korean War, 1950-1953—Personal narratives, American 650 #0$aKorean War, 1950-1953$vPersonal narratives, American
6.	Biological treatment of sewage	Sewage—Purification—Biological treatment 650 #0$aSewage$xPurification$xBiological treatment
7.	Grist for the mill: the flour mills of Brazil	Flour mills – Brazil 650 #0$aFlour mills$zBrazil
8.	Hallelujah I'm a bum: a study of tramps and hoboes	Tramps 650 #0$aTramps
9.	Harrap German-Spanish-German dictionary	1. German language—Dictionaries— Spanish 650 #0$aGerman language$vDictionaries$xSpanish 2. Spanish language—Dictionaries— German 650 #0$aSpanish language$vDictionaries$xGerman
10.	A history of the People's Republic of China from 1950-1975	China—History—1949-1976 650 #0$aChina$xHistory$y1949-1976
11.	House plans by architects	Architecture, Domestic— Designs and plans 650 #0$aArchitecture, Domestic$vDesigns and plans
12.	How real is telekinesis?	Psychokinesis 650 #0$aPsychokinesis
13.	How to tune a French horn	Horn (Musical instrument) —Tuning 650 #0$aHorn (Musical instrument)$xTuning
14.	How to tune a piano	Piano—Tuning 650 #0$aPiano$xTuning
15.	An introduction to Eskimo folksongs	Folk songs, Eskimo 650 #0$aFolk songs, Eskimo

EXERCISE 10.3

1.	Medieval history	Middle Ages—History 650 #0$aMiddle Ages$xHistory
2.	Telephone directory of Columbus, Nebraska	Columbus (Nebr.) – Telephone directories 651 #0$aColumbus (Nebr.)$vTelephone directories
3.	Mendicants: a history of begging	1. Beggars—History 650 #0$aBeggars$xHistory 2. Begging—History 650 #0$aBegging$xHistory
4.	The model ship catalogue	Ship models – Catalogs 650 #0$aShip models$vCatalogs
5.	Negotiation in the hostage situation	Hostage negotiations 650 #0$aHostage negotiations
6.	A new bibliography of fiction about dogs	Dogs—Fiction—Bibliography 650 #0$aDogs$vFiction$vBibliography
7.	The dating of porcelain from China	Porcelain—China—Dating 650 #0$aPorcelain$zChina$xDating
8.	The psychological effects of being unemployed	Unemployment—Psychological aspects 650 #0$aUnemployment$xPsychological aspects
9.	Relations between Judaism and Islam	1. Judaism— Relations—Islam 650 #0$aJudaism$xRelations$xIslam 2. Islam—Relations—Judaism 650 #0$aIslam$xRelations$xJudaism
10.	Rhymes and poetry for children	Children's poetry 650 #0$aChildren's poetry
11.	Corrosion of iron and concrete	1. Iron – Corrosion 650 #0$aIron$xCorrosion 2. Concrete – Corrosion 650 #0$aConcrete$xCorrosion
12.	The story of the Holy Grail	Grail 650 #0$aGrail
13.	Snakes of Kentucky	Snakes – Kentucky 650 #0$aSnakes$zKentucky
14.	A study of parents without partners	Single parents 650 #0$aSingle parents
15.	Surfboard riding in Hawaii	Surfing – Hawaii 650 #0$aSurfing$zHawaii

EXERCISE 10.4

1.	Surgeons in the Argentine Navy (hint: check a name authority file for the correct form of name)	Argentina. Armada – Surgeons 610 10$aArgentina. Armada$xSurgeons
2.	Pilot Creek in Texas	Pilot Grove Creek (Tex.) 651 #0$aPilot Grove Creek (Tex.)
3.	Public access to the Internet in libraries	Internet access for library users 650 #0$aInternet access for library users
4.	Techniques for photographing birds	Photography of birds 650 #0$aPhotography of birds
5.	A collection of original photographs of the Vietnam War (not a book of reproduced photos)	Vietnamese Conflict, 1961-1975 – Photographs 650 #0$aVietnamese Conflict, 1961-1975 $vPhotographs
6.	Television repair manual	Television—Repairing—Handbooks, manuals, etc. 650 #0$aTelevision$xRepairing$vHandbooks, manuals, etc
7.	Public library services to preschoolers	Libraries and preschool children 650 #0$aLibraries and preschool children
8.	Easy dried flower pictures	Preserved flower pictures 650 #0$aPreserved flower pictures
9.	Measuring the earth's gravitational pull	Gravity—Measurement 650 #0$aGravity$xMeasurement
10.	The five commandments of Buddhism	Five Precepts (Buddhism) 650 #0$aFive Precepts (Buddhism)
11.	Judging English riding	Horsemanship—Officiating 650 #0$aHorsemanship$xOfficiating
12.	Transportation of nuclear wastes: legal requirements in Germany	Radioactive wastes – Transportation – Law and legislation – Germany 650 #0$aRadioactive wastes$xTransportation$xLaw and legislation$zGermany
13.	Ice-climbing in Nepal	Snow and ice climbing—Nepal 650 #0$aSnow and ice climbing$zNepal
14.	When your partner dies	1. Widowhood 650 #0$aWidowhood 2. Bereavement 650 #0$aBereavement
15.	Reusing your wastepaper	Waste paper—Recycling 650 #0$aWaste paper$xRecycling

FREE-FLOATING SUBDIVISIONS (H 1095)

Form and Topical Subdivisions of General Application

Scope notes explaining the use of individual subdivisions are given in H 1095 of the *Manual*. Form subdivisions are underlined in the list below.

—Abbreviations

—Abbreviations—Dictionaries

—Abbreviations of titles

—Ability testing *(May Subd Geog)*

—Abstracting and indexing *(May Subd Geog)*

—Abstracts

—Access control *(May Subd Geog)*

—Accidents *(May Subd Geog)*

—Accidents—Investigation *(May Subd Geog)*

—Accounting

—Accreditation *(May Subd Geog)*

—Acronyms

—Acronyms—Dictionaries

—Administration

—Aerial photographs

—Air conditioning *(May Subd Geog)*

—Air conditioning—Control *(May Subd Geog)*

—Amateurs' manuals

—Analysis

—Anecdotes

—Anniversaries, etc.

—Archival resources

—Archives

—Archives—Microform catalogs

—Art

—Atlases

—Audio-visual aids

—Audio-visual aids—Catalogs

—Audiotape catalogs

—Auditing

—Authorship

—Automatic control

—Automation

—Autonomous communities

—Autonomous regions

—Awards *(May Subd Geog)*

—Barrier-free design *(May Subd Geog)*

—Biblical teaching

—Bibliography

—Bibliography—Catalogs

—Bibliography—Early

—Bibliography—Exhibitions

—Bibliography—Methodology

—Bibliography—Microform catalogs

—Bibliography—Union lists

—Bibliography of bibliographies

—Bio-bibliography

—Bio-bibliography—Dictionaries

—Biography

—Biography—Dictionaries

—Biography—Dictionaries—French, [Italian, etc.]

—Biography—History and criticism

—Book reviews

—Buildings

—By-laws

—By-products

—Calendars

—Calibration *(May Subd Geog)*

—Cantons

—Caricatures and cartoons

—Case studies

—Catalogs

—Catalogs and collections *(May Subd Geog)*

—CD-ROM catalogs

—Censorship *(May Subd Geog)*

—Centennial celebrations, etc.

—Certification *(May Subd Geog)*

—Charitable contributions *(May Subd Geog)*

—Charts, diagrams, etc.

—Chronology

—Citizen participation

—Classification

—Cleaning *(May Subd Geog)*

—Code numbers

—Code words

—Cold weather conditions

—Collectibles *(May Subd Geog)*

—Collection and preservation *(May Subd Geog)*

—Collectors and collecting *(May Subd Geog)*

—Colonies

—Comic books, strips, etc.

—Communication systems

—Compact disc catalogs

—Comparative method

—Comparative studies

—Competitions *(May Subd Geog)*

—Composition

—Computer-aided design *(May Subd Geog)*

—Computer-assisted instruction

—Computer games

—Computer network resources

—Computer networks *(May Subd Geog)*

—Computer networks—Security measures *(May Subd Geog)*

—Computer programs

—Computer simulation

—Concordances

—Congresses

—Congresses—Attendance

—Conservation and restoration *(May Subd Geog)*

—Control *(May Subd Geog)*

—Cooling *(May Subd Geog)*

—Corrosion *(May Subd Geog)*

—Corrupt practices *(May Subd Geog)*

—Cost control

—Cost effectiveness

—Cost of operation

—Costs

—Cross-cultural studies

—Cult *(May Subd Geog)*

—Curricula *(May Subd Geog)*

—Customer services *(May Subd Geog)*

—Data processing

—Data tape catalogs

—Databases

—Dating

—Decision making

—Defects *(May Subd Geog)*

—Defects—Reporting *(May Subd Geog)*

—Defense measures *(May Subd Geog)*

—Departments

—Design

—Design and construction

—Design and plans

—Deterioration

—Dictionaries

—Dictionaries—French, [Italian. etc.]

—Dictionaries—Polyglot

—Dictionaries, Juvenile

—Digitization *(May Subd Geog)*

—Directories

—Discipline

—Discography

—Documentation *(May Subd Geog)*

—Drama

—Drawings

—Drying *(May Subd Geog)*

—Dust control *(May Subd Geog)*

—Early works to 1800

—Earthquake effects *(May Subd Geog)*

—Econometric models

—Economic aspects *(May Subd Geog)*

—Electromechanical analogies

—Electronic discussion groups

—Electronic information resources

—Employees

—Encyclopedias

—Encyclopedias, Juvenile

—Endowments

—Energy conservation *(May Subd Geog)*

—Energy consumption *(May Subd Geog)*

—Environmental aspects *(May Subd Geog)*

—Equipment and supplies

—Estimates *(May Subd Geog)*

—Evaluation

—Examinations

—Examinations—Study guides

—Examination, questions, etc.

—Exhibitions

—Experiments

—Expertising *(May Subd Geog)*

—Facsimiles

—Fiction

—Field work

—Film catalogs

—Finance

—Fires and fire prevention *(May Subd Geog)*

—Folklore

—Food service *(May Subd Geog)*

—Forecasting

—Foreign countries

Foreign influences

—Forgeries *(May Subd Geog)*

—Forms

—Fume control *(May Subd Geog)*

—Geographic information systems *(May Subd Geog)*

—Government policy *(May Subd Geog)*

—Grading *(May Subd Geog)*

—Graphic methods

—Guidebooks

—Handbooks, manuals, etc.

—Health aspects *(May Subd Geog)*

—Heating and ventilation *(May Subd Geog)*

—Heating and ventilation—Control *(May Subd Geog)*

—Heraldry

—Historiography

—History

—History—To 1500

—History—16th century

—History—17th century

—History—18th century

—History—19th century

—History—20th century

—History—21st century

—History—Chronology

—History—Philosophy

—History—Sources

—History and criticism

—History of doctrines

—History of doctrines—Early church, ca. 30-600

—History of doctrines—Middle Ages, 600-1500

—History of doctrines—16th century

—History of doctrines—17th century

—History of doctrines—18th century

—History of doctrines—19th century

—History of doctrines—20th century

—History of doctrines—21st century

—Hot weather conditions *(May Subd Geog)*

—Humor

—Identification

—Illustrations

—In art

—Indexes

—Industrial applications *(May Subd Geog)*

—Influence

—Information resources

—Information resources management *(May Subd Geog)*

—Information services

—Information technology *(May Subd Geog)*

—Insignia

—Inspection *(May Subd Geog)*

—Installation *(May Subd Geog)*

—Instruments

—Interactive multimedia

—International cooperation

—Interpretation

—Inventories

—Inventory control *(May Subd Geog)*

—Job descriptions *(May Subd Geog)*

—Juvenile drama

—Juvenile fiction

—Juvenile films

—Juvenile humor

—Juvenile literature

—Juvenile poetry

—Juvenile software

—Juvenile sound recordings

—Labeling *(May Subd Geog)*

—Labor productivity *(May Subd Geog)*

—Laboratory manuals

—Landscape architecture *(May Subd Geog)*

—Language

—Legends

—Library resources

—Licenses *(May Subd Geog)*

—Licenses—Fees *(May Subd Geog)*

—Lighting *(May Subd Geog)*

—Linear programming

—Literary collections

—Liturgy

—Liturgy—Texts

—Location *(May Subd Geog)*

—Longitudinal studies

—Maintenance and repair

—Management

—Manuscripts

—Manuscripts—Catalogs

—Manuscripts—Facsimiles

—Manuscripts—Indexes

—Manuscripts—Microform catalogs

—Maps

—Maps—Bibliography

—Maps—Early works to 1800

—Maps—Facsimiles

—Maps—Symbols

—Maps, Comparative

—Maps, Manuscript

—Maps, Mental

—Maps, Outline and base

—Maps, Physical

—Maps, Pictorial

—Maps, Topographic

—Maps, Tourist

—Maps for children

—Maps for people with visual disabilities

—Maps for the blind

Marketing

—Materials

—Mathematical models

—Mathematics

—Measurement

—Medals *(May Subd Geog)*

—Medical examinations *(May Subd Geog)*

—Meditations

—Membership

—Methodology

—Microform catalogs

—Miscellanea

—Models *(May Subd Geog)*

—Moisture *(May Subd Geog)*

—Moral and ethical aspects *(May Subd Geog)*

—Museums *(May Subd Geog)*

—Mythology *(May Subd Geog)*

—Name

—Names

—Newspapers

—Noise

—Nomenclature

—Nomograms

—Notation

—Observations

—Observers' manuals

—Officials and employees

—On postage stamps

—Orbit

—Outlines, syllabi, etc.

—Packaging *(May Subd Geog)*

—Packing *(May Subd Geog)*

—Pamphlets

—Papal documents

—Parodies, imitations, etc.

—Passenger lists

—Patents

—Periodicals

—Periodicals—Abbreviations of titles

—Periodicals—Bibliography

—Periodicals—Bibliography—Catalogs

—Periodicals—Bibliography—Union lists

—Periodicals—Indexes

—Personal narratives

—Personal narratives—History and criticism

—Personnel management

—Philosophy

—Photographs

—Photographs from space

—Physiological aspects

—Physiological effect

—Pictorial works

—Planning

—Poetry

—Political activity

—Political aspects *(May Subd Geog)*

—Popular works

—Posters

—Power supply *(May Subd Geog)*

—Practice *(May Subd Geog)*

—Prayer-books and devotions

—Prayer-books and devotions—History and criticism

—Preservation *(May Subd Geog)*

—Press coverage *(May Subd Geog)*

—Prevention

—Prices *(May Subd Geog)*

—Prices—Government policy *(May Subd Geog)*

—Private collections *(May Subd Geog)*

—Privileges and immunities

—<u>Problems, exercises, etc.</u>

—Production and direction *(May Subd Geog)*

—Production control *(May Subd Geog)*

—Production standards *(May Subd Geog)*

—<u>Programmed instruction</u>

—Programming *(May Subd Geog)*

—Prophecies

—Protection *(May Subd Geog)*

—Provinces

—Psychological aspects

—Psychology

—Public opinion

—Public relations *(May Subd Geog)*

—Publishing *(May Subd Geog)*

—Purchasing *(May Subd Geog)*

—Quality control

—<u>Quotations, maxims, etc.</u>

—Rates *(May Subd Geog)*

—<u>Records and correspondence</u>

—Recreational use *(May Subd Geog)*

—Reference books

—Regional disparities

—Regions

—<u>Registers</u>

—Reliability

—Religion

—Remodeling *(May Subd Geog)*

—Remote sensing

—<u>Remote-sensing maps</u>

—Repairing *(May Subd Geog)*

—Republics

—Research *(May Subd Geog)*

—Research grants *(May Subd Geog)*

—<u>Reviews</u>

—Risk assessment *(May Subd Geog)*

—<u>Romances</u>

—<u>Rules</u>

—<u>Rules and practice</u>

—Safety appliances *(May Subd Geog)*

—Safety measures

—Safety regulations *(May Subd Geog)*

—Sanitation *(May Subd Geog)*

—Scholarships, fellowships, etc. *(May Subd Geog)*

—Scientific applications *(May Subd Geog)*

—Security measures *(May Subd Geog)*

—<u>Sermons</u>

—Sermons—History and criticism

—Sex differences

—Simulation methods

—Slang

—<u>Slides</u>

—Social aspects *(May Subd Geog)*

—Societies, etc.

—Sociological aspects

—<u>Software</u>

—<u>Songs and music</u>

—Songs and music—Discography

—Songs and music—History and criticism

—<u>Songs and music—Texts</u>

—Soundproofing *(May Subd Geog)*

—<u>Sources</u>

—<u>Specifications</u> *(May Subd Geog)*

—<u>Specimens</u>

—Spectra

—Speeches in Congress

—Stability

—Standards *(May Subd Geog)*

—State supervision

—States

—Statistical methods

—Statistical services

—Statistics

—Storage *(May Subd Geog)*

—Study and teaching *(May Subd Geog)*

—Study and teaching—Activity programs *(May Subd Geog)*

—Study and teaching—Audio-visual aids

—Study and teaching—Simulation methods

—Study and teaching—Supervision *(May Subd Geog)*

—Study and teaching (Continuing education) *(May Subd Geog)*

—Study and teaching (Continuing education)—Audio-visual aids

—Study and teaching (Early childhood) *(May Subd Geog)*

—Study and teaching (Early childhood)—Activity programs *(May Subd Geog)*

—Study and teaching (Early childhood)—Audio-visual aids

—Study and teaching (Elementary) *(May Subd Geog)*

—Study and teaching (Elementary)—Activity programs *(May Subd Geog)*

—Study and teaching (Elementary)—Audio-visual aids

—Study and teaching (Elementary)—Simulation methods

—Study and teaching (Graduate) *(May Subd Geog)*

—Study and teaching (Higher) *(May Subd Geog)*

—Study and teaching (Higher)—Activity programs *(May Subd Geog)*

—Study and teaching (Higher)—Audio-visual aids

—Study and teaching (Higher)—Simulation methods

—Study and teaching (Internship) *(May Subd Geog)*

—Study and teaching (Middle school) *(May Subd Geog)*

—Study and teaching (Middle school)—Activity programs *(May Subd Geog)*

—Study and teaching (Middle school)—Audio-visual aids

—Study and teaching (Preschool) *(May Subd Geog)*

—Study and teaching (Preschool)—Activity programs *(May Subd Geog)*

—Study and teaching (Preschool)—Audio-visual aids

—Study and teaching (Primary) *(May Subd Geog)*

—Study and teaching (Primary)—Activity programs *(May Subd Geog)*

—Study and teaching (Primary)—Audio-visual aids

—Study and teaching (Residency) *(May Subd Geog)*

—Study and teaching (Secondary) *(May Subd Geog)*

—Study and teaching (Secondary)—Activity programs *(May Subd Geog)*

—Study and teaching (Secondary)—Audio-visual aids

—Study and teaching (Secondary)—Simulation methods

—Study guides

—Tables

—Tables of contents

—Taxation *(May Subd Geog)*

—Taxation-Law and legislation *(May Subd Geog)*

—Technique

—Technological innovations *(May Subd Geog)*

—Telephone directories

—Terminology

—Terminology—Pronunciation

—Territories and possessions

—Testing

—Textbooks

—Texts

—Themes, motives

—Therapeutic use *(May Subd Geog)*

—Tombs *(May Subd Geog)*

—Toxicology *(May Subd Geog)*

—Trademarks

—Translating *(May Subd Geog)*

—Translations

—Translations into [name of language]

—Transportation *(May Subd Geog)*

—Tropical conditions

—Union lists

—Union territories

—Use studies

—Validity *(May Subd Geog)*

—Valuation *(May Subd Geog)*

—Vibration *(May Subd Geog)*

—Video catalogs

—Vocational guidance *(May Subd Geog)*

—Waste disposal *(May Subd Geog)*

—Waste minimization *(May Subd Geog)*

—Water-supply

—Weblogs

—Weight

—Weights and measures

GLOSSARY

This glossary contains the main terms used in the book. For a comprehensive glossary, see Mortimer, Mary, *LibrarySpeak: a glossary of terms in librarianship and information management.*

AACR2R *See* Anglo-American Cataloguing Rules Second edition 2002 revision

ABN *See* Australian Bibliographic Network

access point A heading given to a catalog or database record or entry in a bibliography which enables a user to find the item

added entry Any entry, other than the main entry (and subject entries), by which the user can access the catalog; e.g., title, joint author, illustrator, editor, compiler, translator, series, corporate body

Anglo-American Cataloguing Rules Second edition 2002 revision Revision in 2002 of a set of rules for descriptive cataloging developed by the Library Association (Great Britain) and the American Library Association, and published in 1967 in separate British and North American texts; revised into one consolidated text in 1978 (Anglo-American Cataloguing Rules Second Edition - AACR2); revised in 1988, 1998 and 2002. Adopted by major libraries in most English-speaking countries, and translated into many other languages

author The person chiefly responsible for the intellectual or artistic content of a work; e.g., writer of a book, compiler of a bibliography, composer of a musical work, artist, photographer

authorized heading *See* preferred term

authority control The control of access points by establishing and using consistent headings

authority file A collection of authority records containing the preferred forms of headings for names, series and subjects. It can be on cards, microfiche or online

authority record A record of the preferred heading for a person, place, corporate body, series or title and the references to and from the heading

authority work The establishment and maintenance of authority files

bibliographic record A catalog entry in card, microtext, machine-readable or other form containing full cataloging information for a given item

biography 1. A written account of a person's life. 2. The branch of literature concerned with people's individual lives

Boolean logic Use of the terms AND, OR, NOT to formulate online search commands, to represent any logical possibility

Boolean operator **And**: retrieves only items with both terms. **Or**: retrieves items with either term. **Not**: retrieves items with one term and not the other. These words are used in the formulation of search strategies for the retrieval of online information

broader term, broader topic BT. A more general subject heading

BT *See* broader term, broader topic

catalog A list of library materials contained in a collection, a library or a group of libraries, arranged according to some definite plan

cataloger A person who prepares catalog entries and maintains a catalog so that library materials can be retrieved efficiently

cataloging The preparation of bibliographic information for catalog records. Cataloging consists of descriptive cataloging, subject cataloging and classification

cataloging-in-publication CIP. Cataloging data produced by the national library or other agency of the country of publication, included in the work when it is published

cataloging tools Publications of the international cataloging rules and standards, including *Anglo-American cataloguing rules (AACR), Library of Congress subject headings (LCSH), Library of Congress classification (LCC), Dewey decimal classification (DDC)*

chronological subdivision *See* period subdivision

CIP *See* cataloging-in-publication

classification number Number allocated to a library item to indicate a subject

collocation Arrangement that locates like material together

controlled vocabulary Terms found in an authoritative list of terms—e.g., Library of Congress Subject Headings, a database thesaurus

corporate body An organization or group of people identified by a particular name, and acting as an entity

cross reference *See* reference

database A collection of records in machine-readable format, each record being the required information about one item

descriptor A term used to identify a subject

dictionary catalog A catalog with all the entries arranged in a single alphabetical sequence

direct entry A heading using the specific term that describes the topic—e.g., Red fescue

direct subdivision A subdivision that directly follows the main heading or subdivision. Usually used for geographic subdivisions

encyclopaedia A systematic summary of all significant knowledge; a summary of the knowledge of one subject. Usually arranged alphabetically

explanatory reference A longer "see" or "see also" reference that explains when a heading or headings should be used

foreword A brief statement of the reasons for the book, usually by the author or editor. It appears after the title page and before the introduction

form 1. The way in which a bibliographic work is arranged—e.g., dictionary. 2. Type of literary work—e.g., poetry, drama

format 1. Appearance and make-up of a book; its size, paper, type, binding etc. 2. Physical type of an audiovisual item—e.g., slide, filmstrip etc. 3. Physical organization of a catalog—e.g., card, microfiche, online etc

form heading A heading that represents the physical, bibliographic, artistic or literary form of a work—e.g., Encyclopedias, Dictionaries, Short stories

form subdivision A subdivision that brings out the form of a work, e.g., **—Periodicals, —Bibliography**

free-floating subdivision A subdivision that may be used under any existing appropriate LC subject heading

free text vocabulary *See* uncontrolled vocabulary

general reference A reference made to a group of headings, rather than one specific heading—e.g., Woodworking industries - *SA names of specific industries, e.g.* Furniture industry and trade. Cf specific reference

geographic heading Place name used as a subject heading

geographic name Name of a place—country, state, city, town, suburb etc

geographic qualifier The name of a larger geographic entity added to a local place name—e.g., Phoenix (Ariz.)

geographic subdivision Place name used as a subdivision of a topic

hierarchy A system of organization in which narrower topics are part of broader topics

homograph A word that looks the same as another, but has a different meaning

homonym A word that sounds the same as another, and may be spelt the same, but has a different meaning

index 1. An alphabetical list of terms or topics in a work, usually found at the back. 2. A systematically arranged list that indicates the contents of a document or group of documents

indirect subdivision A subdivision in which another element is interposed between the main heading and the specific subdivision. Usually used for geographic subdivisions

initial article The word that introduces a noun at the beginning of a title—e.g., the, a, an

inverted heading A heading in which the normal order of the words is reversed, in order to group like terms together in the subject list—e.g., Cookery, French

journal A periodical issued by an institution, corporation or learned society containing current information and reports of activities or works in a particular field

jurisdictional heading A geographic heading used for a political jurisdiction, that is the name of an area used to represent a government

keyword A significant term found in a document that identifies subject content

LC *See* Library of Congress

LCSH *See* Library of Congress Subject Headings

Library of Congress The library of the United States Congress; the de facto national library of the United States

Library of Congress Subject Headings The authoritative list of subject headings compiled and maintained by the Library of Congress

literary warrant The volume of books written, or likely to be written, on a topic

monograph A publication either complete in one part or in a finite number of separate parts

multiple subdivision A subdivision that is used to show the creation of similar subdivisions under the same heading, e.g., —Religious aspects—Buddhism, [Christianity, etc.]

name authority file A collection of authority records containing the preferred forms of headings for names, including personal and corporate names. It can be on cards, microfiche or online

narrower term, narrower topic NT. A more specific subject heading

natural language *See* uncontrolled vocabulary

non-jurisdictional heading A geographic heading used for a place other than a political jurisdiction—e.g., Great Barrier Reef, Sydney Harbour Bridge

non-preferred term Also unauthorized heading. A term that is not taken from an authorized list of headings and should not be used

NT *See* narrower term, narrower topic

other title information Also subtitle. Title on an item other than the title proper or parallel or series title; also any phrase appearing in conjunction with the title proper

pattern heading A heading that serves as a model of subdivisions for headings in the same category—e.g., the pattern of subdivisions for 'Foot' can be followed for any similar part of the body

periodical A serial with a distinctive title intended to appear in successive parts at stated and regular intervals. Often used as a synonym for serial

period subdivision Also chronological subdivision. A subdivision that shows the period or span of time covered by a work, or the period in which the work appeared

phrase heading A heading consisting of a group of words

post-coordinate Of subject headings or other search terms, put together by the user at the time of searching. Refers to terms used for searching an online index or database, where the computer combines the terms to carry out the search

pre-coordinate Of subject headings or other search terms, put together by the cataloger or indexer

preface The author's or editor's reasons for the book. It appears after the title page and before the introduction

preferred term Also authorized heading. A term taken from an authorized list of headings and used in a catalog

qualifier An addition to a name etc enclosed in parentheses

reference A direction from one heading to another

related term, related topic RT. A subject heading at the same level of specificity to another heading and related in subject matter

retrospective conversion Changing older records, usually into machine-readable form

RT *See* related term, related topic

SA *See* see also reference

scan 1. To examine every item in a collection to determine usefulness for information retrieval. 2. To read a printed document into a computer

scope note A note describing the range and meaning of a subject heading

search strategy 1. The approach adopted to finding information on a particular topic. 2. The search statements used to answer an enquiry

search term A word, phrase or number entered by a user to find the records on a database that match the term

see also reference A direction from one heading to another when both are used

see reference Also USE reference. A direction from one heading that is not used to another heading which is used

serial A publication issued in successive parts and intended to be continued indefinitely

specific reference A reference from one heading to another. Cf general reference

subdivision An extension of a subject heading that indicates an aspect - form, topic, place or period

subject analysis Identification of the intellectual content of a work

subject authority file A file of all the subject headings used in the catalog, and the relevant references

subject authority record A record of a subject heading that shows the preferred form, the authority used to determine the heading and the references to and from the heading in the catalog

subject cataloging Describing the content of a work using subject headings

subject entry An entry under the heading for the subject

subject heading A heading that describes a subject and provides subject access to a catalog

subordinate body A corporate body that is part of a larger corporate body

subtitle *See* other title information

summary Also abstract. A summary of the essential points of an article or literary work

synonym A word with the same meaning as another

thesaurus 1. A work containing synonymous and related words and phrases. 2. A list of controlled terms used in a database

title A word or phrase that names the item

title proper The main name of an item, including alternative title/s but excluding parallel titles and other title information

topical heading A heading that represents a subject or topic

topical subdivision A subdivision that represents an aspect of the main subject other than form, period or place

UF *See* USED FOR reference

unauthorized heading *See* non-preferred term

uncontrolled vocabulary Also natural language, free text vocabulary. Terms taken directly from the work, without reference to a list of subject headings, thesaurus or authority file

USED FOR reference UF. The notation used with a preferred heading, which shows the non-preferred heading so that a *see* reference can be made—e.g., "Capture at sea—UF Maritime capture" means that **Capture at sea** is the preferred heading, not **Maritime capture**

USE reference *See* see reference

vocabulary control Restriction of the terms in a catalog, bibliography or index to those taken from a list of subject headings or thesaurus

INDEX

BIBLIOGRAPHY

Chan, Lois Mai, *Library of Congress subject headings: principles and application* 4th ed., Westport, Conn., Libraries Unlimited, 2005.

Langridge, D. W., *Subject analysis: principles and procedures*, London, Bowker-Saur, 1989.

Library of Congress, *Cataloging service bulletin,* Washington, D.C., Library of Congress.

Library of Congress, *Free-floating subdivisions: an alphabetical index,* Washington, D.C., Library of Congress.

Library of Congress, *Library of Congress subject headings,* various editions, Washington, D.C., Library of Congress.

Library of Congress, *Subject cataloging manual: subject headings* 5th ed., Washington, D.C., Library of Congress, 1996 onwards, with half-yearly updates.

Olson, Hope A. and John J. Boll, *Subject analysis in online catalogs* 2nd ed., Englewood, Colo., Libraries Unlimited, 2001.

LIBRARY EDUCATION SERIES

This series of paperback workbooks introduces skills needed by library science students and library technicians, as well as librarians seeking refresher materials or study guides for in-service training classes. Each book teaches essential professional skills in a step-by-step process, accompanied by numerous practical examples, exercises and quizzes to reinforce learning, and an appropriate glossary.

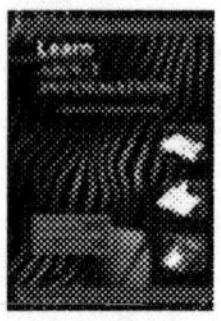

Learn About Information
First North American Edition ©2007
Mary Gosling, Elizabeth Hopgood and Karen Lochhead
ISBN: 978-1-59095-801-8 Paperback, 217 pp.
$37.99

Learn Basic Library Skills
Second North American Edition ©2007
Elaine Anderson, Mary Gosling and Mary Mortimer
ISBN: 978-1-59095-802-5 Paperback, 230 pp.,
$42.99

Learn Descriptive Cataloging
Second North American Edition ©2007
Mary Mortimer
ISBN: 978-1-59095-803-2 Paperback, 281 pp.
$37.99

Learn Dewey Decimal Classification (Edition 22)
First North American Edition ©2007
Mary Mortimer
ISBN: 978-1-59095-804-9 Paperback, 135 pp.
$37.99

Learn Library Management
Second North American Edition ©2007
Bob Pymm and Damon D. Hickey
ISBN: 978-1-59095-805-6 Paperback, 189 pp.
$37.99

Learn Library of Congress Classification
Second Edition ©2007
Helena Dittman and Jane Hardy
ISBN: 978-1-59095-806-3 Paperback, 161 pp.
$37.99

Printed in the United States
99031LV00003B